DEDICATION

For my grandmother, Jenny Hicks Heller,

my mother, Arlene Geiger Heller,

and my firstborn daughter, Heather Dawn Ecklund

Your lives and deaths have enriched the soil of my soul,

seeding new life on this side of the threshold.

CONTENTS

ACKNOWLEDGMENTS

Thanks to my editor, Carolyn Kott Washburne, who found herself editing through teary eyes on more than one occasion. I would also like to thank Edward Schultz, Lisa Henner, and my fellow writers of the Driftless Writing Center for their feedback and encouragement.

This book has been a labor of love for many years, and is possible only because of the willingness of the contributors to share their life-changing and intimate experiences with you, the reader. I am deeply grateful to have been the caretaker of these precious stories. I now release them, like seeds on the wind, to find new life as you plant them into your own hearts. I look forward to seeing what grows.

There is a grave, too, in each

survivor. By it, the dead one lives.

He enters us, a broken blade,

sharp, clear as a lens or mirror.

And he comes into us helpless, tender

as the newborn enter the world. Great

is the burden of our care. We must be true

to ourselves. How else will he know us?

Like a wound, grief receives him.

Like graves, we heal over, and yet keep

as part of ourselves the severe gift.

By grief, more inward than darkness,

the dead become the intelligence of life.

Where the tree falls, the forest rises.

There is nowhere to stand but in absence,

no life but in the fateful light.

                                        --Wendell Berry

INTRODUCTION

When I learned my mother was dying, I wondered how her death would change my life. I'd known people whose mother had died, but I hadn't really talked to them in depth. Opportunities to have those conversations had been there; I was either unsure how to do it, or just unwilling to listen.

The idea for this book came as I learned to listen to the powerful stories told by family and friends following the death of a loved one. There is an honesty, intimacy, tenderness, and even hopefulness in the telling of and listening to such stories. The masks drop, we allow ourselves to be vulnerable, and we speak heart to heart. How could it be that talking about death could be so life affirming?

More people should hear these life-giving death stories, I thought. Wouldn't it be wonderful to publish a collection of stories, told in the first person, through the eyes and in the words of those who experienced them? Could that make it easier for the rest of us to talk about death?

It was just an idea, and I harbored it silently, planting the seed in the darkness away from the light. Slowly, oh so slowly, it germinated. A little sprout rose above the surface, and I started talking about the idea to a few friends and to my writers group, all of whom encouraged me to pursue the project.

I struggled to define just what kind of stories I was looking for until I discovered Wendell Berry's poem "The Rising." When I read the line "Where the tree falls, the forest rises," I realized it was stories of death *and renewal* I was looking for and began to ask for them. People I knew and people I didn't know began to send them. From all walks of life they told of fathers, mothers, daughters, sons, grandchildren, in-laws, friends, and others whose lives and deaths planted in them a new way of being, a renewed perspective. Some stories were fairly recent, some still uncovering new meaning after many years. They are each unique yet universal.

Though I have read these stories numerous times now, they never fail to move me. Savor them slowly. My hope is that through reading them, you, the reader will experience their transformative power and be empowered to share your own stories of loss and renewal, whether in person or in prose.

Mary's son, Cullan, revives the woodsman spirit of his late grandfather,
Donald McInnis, in the tall hardwoods of the Harman Nature Reserve
in Cedar Falls, Iowa.

TREES AND FATHERS
MARY MCINNIS

The nice thing about driving while talking is that I don't have to look at my dad. And he doesn't feel obligated to look at me. Mostly we just let our eyes flicker along the tall, white pines reaching up from straight, bare trunks to sparse green arms to snowy scarves to pointed "chook" hats—not too symmetrical, not all "Oh, Tannenbaum," but like they're supposed to be. Cold mornings like this, the boughs sparkle, and for now, we can't see the hospital for the trees.

"1500 an acre now, used to be you could get an acre for a couple hundred bucks," my dad says.

Dad's dad was a woodsman, logging his small plot of land by hand with his only son. But most people in the north woods of Michigan knew Stanley "Mac" McInnis as the sixth grade teacher at the Powers Elementary School. And the janitor. And the principal. Yesterday I came right out and asked my dad what his father died of, not staring out this windshield, but staring across the living room at the decorative alcove my dad had built 35 years ago, when I was born. That alcove was an inside joke, with hidden sliding doors for Old Fashioned mix and Johnny Walker Scotch.

"Ulcer," my dad had said from his spot to my right on the couch, acting as if he didn't know why I was asking. Maybe he didn't. But we talked about the grandfather I'd never met for quite a while then, the man who had lived 30 miles from the clear-cut lot my dad eventually built our home on. My grandfather had died of an ulcer at a time when there was no Tagamet or Prilosec. Was there any connection, I wondered, in my dad becoming a pharmacist? I looked away from the alcove to my mother, standing at the kitchen sink. She has an ulcer now. Me, I just throw my body against stuck car doors every now and then. Hard.

The pines lining the road are like blinders, directing us, filtering out anything that falls short of meaningful. Our conversation is overseen by these grand guides.

"So, Dad, what did your dad's dad do?" I ask him now with feigned ease, without a glance.

"He was a woodsman, too. Andrew McInnis. He bought stumpage and had a team of horses to drag the logs out."

"Stumpage?" I ask.

"Yeah, he owned the trees on the land, but not the land," Dad says.

I listen as he talks of floating the huge pines down rivers to lake Michigan, then onto barges bound for Chicago, and I feel a twinge of sadness, of loss.

"Most of the lumber used to build up Chicago came from the Upper Peninsula," he says.

"What did my great-grandpa think about reforestation?" I ask.

Dad laughs. "That wasn't exactly a priority back then," he says with a smile I can feel. The environment. We both respect it completely, I know, even if he is a Republican.

"What about Grandma's parents? What did they do?" I ask, a little too forced, a poor transition, the urgency surely apparent. Like when I said to him on my last visit, then instantly regretted in the silence that followed—"Don't wait to do anything." That's what hospice will tell you.

But Dad continues on, wearing the green-and-red chook his mother knit him, stretched over his balding head and surgical scar. All I can see in my peripheral vision, though, is the loosely knit fabric of my French-Canadian woodsman heritage.

"Felix Poquette was a woodsman, too. The kind that went off to logging camp for months. Then he'd come home for a few weeks, just enough time to leave his wife pregnant," he chuckles. They had seven kids, I learn. I note the names, thinking about my baby sister hoping to get pregnant now, so Dad can see her firstborn. Adelphis, Leonard, Fred, Arthur . . . maybe she will have a girl . . . Lillian, May, Vina.

The trip to my dad's radiation session is a stretch of pines and questions. Soon I find amid the trees that I'm comfortable with these questions, and the intentions behind them. He will be gone soon, and we both know it. Do the trees, I wonder?

16

"Dad, is there anything you wish you would have done, or still want to do?" I ask him.

"No. I think I've had a pretty good life. A nice family, you four daughters, a comfortable life. I'm not one of these guys who's gonna yell at God about it not being fair," he says.

He tells me about how he went to the ear doctor for a regular check-up, and the doctor said, "I hope I'm not crossing a line here or anything, but I've never seen such a thing. You seem to be handling this so well."

Dad and I joke about how he should take up writing, penning a *Tuesdays with Morrie* kind of thing, only from Morrie's perspective. He's heard of the book but hasn't read it. I own it on a shelf somewhere, sitting, waiting. I have to remember to send it to him. (What I am surprised to find out later, after he reads and returns the book to me, is that he related to Mitch Albom, not Morrie.)

The pines are so tall, not like everything else that shrinks when you return home. They are the real thing. Steady. These guides take us in again, and the conversation turns.

My dad once had the opportunity to buy a plot of wooded land on Lake Superior, 200 feet of frontage, with a ramshackle old "camp" on it. I imagine it dappled with these pines. He watched it in the paper for weeks, "$8,000," and one day it wasn't listed any more.

"I always kind of thought I'd retire on a piece of land in the woods like that," he says.

"Yeah, I've been really feeling something . . . like a pull . . . being here in all these trees again," I say. I talk about possibly buying a piece of this for myself. Then I waver, voicing my fear of seclusion, my need to be near people. If it wasn't for that . . . .

"Oh, invite people over, give anyone an excuse and they'd be out to visit you. Everyone wants to get away," he says.

"You know, I hiked through the Boundary Waters for a week once, and what I really remember is the sound of the trees. I never hear them now. But the wind coming through them was like energy. Energy that I was a part of . . . " I say, trailing off. I don't expect a response, maybe just a raised eyebrow. But I'm wrong.

"Yeah, I really love being way out in the woods. Some hunters never leave sight of the truck. I can't understand that. Me and the guys I hunted with, we'd go off by ourselves, into the real woods. It's different out there. If you stay too close to the truck, you really miss out." Out of the corner of my eye, I see his chook shaking side-to-side.

"There's something about the woods that makes you realize what's important or something," I say, hearing my self-conscious words. I am a 10-year-old daddy's girl again.

"Yup," he says.

We think together, talking every now and then, about these woods. I feel the oxygen they have made taking over my chest, oddly heavy air. My dad's hunting career came to an abrupt end 19 years ago when a stroke left him walking with a cane and unable to support the barrel of a gun without tipping over. He still went to camp with his buddies, though, but I wonder how far he was able to get from the truck.

I tell my dad about my theory of life continuing on like energy, all around us, in the trees. Or something.

"Yeah, who knows, eh? But that hell stuff . . . I'm not so sure about that," he laughs. He's a Catholic, but a thoughtful one.

"Yeah, I'm not sure about anything," I join in, able to laugh at myself, acknowledging how ridiculous any theory on "the after life" really is.

"Want me to send you a little message, Mary? A little bit of brimstone—"

"No way!" I cut him off. That kind of thing would scare the pants off of 10-year-old Mary, and he knows it. I say it before I have time to realize that I do want him to send me a message. But it's too late to say anything now, and the mood is so wonderfully light.

We talk more about the woods, and he tells me if I don't buy some land soon, I'll regret it.

"I'll do it, Dad. Maybe that parcel nearby on the Montreal River," I say.

My husband and I walk through the recently logged 40 acres of land where the Montreal River flows through. The trees are scrubby, not tall pines, not at all majestic. They make no sound. Even with leaves, they'd barely rustle. My legs hurt from the snowy trek, but they manage to carry me out of the barren land.

I take my children to the Hartman Nature Reserve near my new home in Iowa, tall hardwoods all around. The kids are pretending the snow is ice cream on sticks. I stand in the sun that streams through the snowy trees. I hear something. An animal up high? I see no trace of movement. The noise reaches me again. It's the trees. They are creaking. Slow movements of dead branches against live ones. And I know that this is our secret. From now on, in the woods in the dead of winter, I will always hear this sound.

MARY MCINNIS is a writer and a yogi. Her work has appeared in *Counterpunch, Lyrical Iowa, Science & Spirit,* and *Bad Subjects,* among others. Mary started practicing yoga to cope with her father's terminal brain tumor diagnosis in 2003. She now owns a studio in Cedar Falls, Iowa, where she integrates two authentic means of expression, verbal and physical. She knows her father would be very proud of her, although he wouldn't come right out and say it.

Charlene Elderkin and her mother, Arlene Heller

"Mom's openness about her impending death was a great gift for all of our family. It allowed us to speak openly about what was happening; very little was taboo."

MONDAYS WITH MOM

CHARLENE ELDERKIN

For a few short months in the fall of 2003, Mondays were my day to spend with my mother, Arlene Heller. She had been through the ups and downs of treatment for chronic lymphocytic leukemia for several years, with numerous close calls alternating with periods of health and vigor. The bag of tricks was empty now. There weren't any more curative treatments the doctor could offer, so Mom began receiving hospice care at home.

Two of my sisters, Sherri and Jacqui, were living with Mom and Dad, helping out with the day-to-day tasks. Living two hours away, I wasn't on hand very much, but I arranged to come once a week to give my sisters a night off and spend time with Mom.

Arlene had grown up on a farm during the depression. The third of 10 children, she and her siblings were given jobs as soon as they could walk. That must be where her work ethic came from, and her obsession with having enough food in the house. Now, people seem to have the impression that I'm a busy person, but they didn't know my mother. The only time she didn't work outside the home was when five of her seven children were under the age of five, including a set of twins. Even then she took in ironing or provided childcare.

When the youngest ones entered school, Mom went back to work in a big way. Her day started at 5 a.m. with an early morning paper route. She was a crossing guard, so three times a day she would be at the corner making sure the kiddies got safely across the street. In between her crossing guard shifts, she did home health care. In the evenings, she cleaned an office building. Did I mention the foster children? And the three children she and Dad (Doyle) adopted? You get the picture.

Mom was big on having enough food. She and Dad grew large vegetable gardens in the summer, helped along with child labor, of course. She baked 12 loaves of bread at a time, and taught us all how to can. Pears, peaches, applesauce, chicken, tomatoes, pickles, beets, plus freezing corn, peach/blueberry pie filling, jams, green beans; we had a chest freezer and countless shelves in the basement stuffed full of food.

But I learned my greatest lessons from Arlene in her last months of life. She accepted her death fearlessly, with a presence that amazes me to this day. Mom saw her illness as a blessing. She had certain things she wanted to get done before she journeyed on, like dictating her personal life history and finishing quilts so each of her grandchildren would have one of their own. She told me she would never have stopped working long enough to do these things if she hadn't gotten sick.

So I came every Monday, staying until Tuesday evening. Mom and I sorted through multiple boxes of photos, organizing and identifying who was who in the pictures. We went through the personal history that she had dictated and my sister had transcribed, making additions and corrections, getting a more complete picture of the life she'd lived.

One Monday, as I was coming through the door, I heard Mom on the phone. She looked really tired, but she had a quilt spread out on the kitchen table that she was tying—the last quilt she'd planned to do. The caller must have asked her what she was doing, because I heard her say, "I'm finishing this quilt so I can die!"

Mom's openness about her impending death was a great gift for all of our family. It allowed us to speak openly about what was happening; very little was taboo. On one visit, she was very excited about having just picked out her coffin, "with pink flowers! I picked out Doyle's, too; he wouldn't be able to do that on his own." And she made sure Dad had a new suit to wear for the funeral, took care of the legal and financial matters with the estate, and had a new photograph taken of the two of them.

Getting things done was what she normally did. What she added to that now was an introspection and self-reflection that I hadn't seen before. She made peace, she apologized, she expressed regret, she professed love and confidence in her children. She was sometimes tired or cranky, sometimes impatient that dying was taking so long, but she was never afraid of death.

On the Sunday before her death, Mom had a fall and couldn't get up, so she was taken to the hospital to make sure she hadn't injured herself. When everything checked out okay, the hospice nurse arranged for her transfer to the inpatient hospice center.

When my daughter Deborah and I arrived at the hospital that Monday, Mom was in a cheery mood. She was singing a little song she'd made up, "I'm gonna die with curly hair!" She was really pleased that she would die with her hair looking good! When the ambulance came to transfer her to the hospice center, the friendly ambulance attendants told her, "You're going to the Hilton!" Deborah rode with her grandmother in the ambulance; Dad and I followed in our respective cars.

Once there, I could see why they had called it "the Hilton." There was a large, open foyer with a grand piano, several fully furnished kitchen/family rooms, a chapel, a playroom for little ones, and a well-stocked library. Mom's room was much larger than the hospital rooms, which makes a big difference with a big family like ours. Her room had a stereo system, desk, sofa bed, and large, private bathroom. Sliding glass doors led out to a private patio facing the hibernating gardens.

Deborah and I stayed over that night on the sofa bed. Mom woke up often throughout the night, trying several times to get out of her bed and sit in a chair, but she fell each time. She didn't have the strength any more.

While it is possible, in retrospect, to romanticize her preparations for death, the last few days were just plain hard—for Mom and all of the family. At one point she declared, "I'm going to tell Heavenly Father that this isn't much fun!"

I went home on Tuesday and returned to the hospice center on Thursday, where four of my siblings and Dad had gathered. Mom had been in a coma all day. Unsure if we were going to get to talk with her again, we wheeled her bed into the foyer. With Dad accompanying us on the grand piano, we sang every song we could remember while mother slept.

On Friday, Mother woke up, and in between the periods of rest visited with us. More family members arrived or were on their way from various parts of the country. I was considering going back to Mom and Dad's for the night to get a shower and a good night's sleep when my brother Fred called to talk to Mom.

She wasn't able to hold the phone on her own, so Dad held it up to her ear. Fred was explaining that he wasn't going to arrive until the following morning. Mom replied,

"I'm not going to be here."

She said it in such a matter-of-fact way that I knew she knew this was it. I decided I would stay the night, after all.

We sang more songs—this time it was Christmas songs, there in her room. As it grew late, everyone went home except my brother Clark and me. Around midnight, my sister Ashley arrived from Utah and was able to have a short visit with Mom. The staff set up a cot next to Mom's bed in addition to the sofa bed so there would be a place for all of us to lie down in the room. In the early morning hours, she slept soundly as we listened to the rhythm of her breath. Mom passed on about 5:45 a.m., November 8, 2003.

I was both stunned and deeply moved when Fred, in Arlene's eulogy, related how he had prayed at 5:30 a.m. for her to be released, even if he couldn't be there. My sister Alisa, who was spending the night in a motel with her husband and children en route, woke up at 5:45 a.m. and knew Mom had passed on. My daughter Amanda, in California, also woke up at the very time of her grandmother's death, knowing she was gone. How deeply connected we all are!

I learned many things from my mother throughout my lifetime, but her final months taught me about life and death in a powerful way that stands out far above everything else. If I can find the strength and peace within myself that she modeled, to face death without fear, I will have learned the greatest lesson from my remarkable mother and teacher, Arlene.

One year after her mother's death, Charlene Elderkin became a hospice volunteer. She cofounded the Threshold Care Circle in 2006, one of the first home funeral educational organizations in the Midwest, and is now a member of the National Home Funeral Alliance. She is currently a student of the Chalice of Repose Project in the Contemplative Musicianship Program, and hopes to provide prescriptive music with voice and harp for the dying after completing further training.

The Wilkins children, from left to right, back row: Nancy, Patricia, Steve, Sheila, front row: Kate holding Patrick, Laura

"When I sang to [Patrick], he always settled right down. My family used to say I was the only one who had this effect upon him, and it was always me my mother called when she needed someone to hold him."

QUIETUS

KATE FITZGERALD

Nine months after my brother died, when I was ten years old, I received a thesaurus for Christmas. Actually, it was a gift for my sister from my mother, and I watched from the sofa while she opened it. "What is it?" I asked.

Sheila, who was a year older than me, put the thick, brown hardcover off to the side on the floor where she sat and turned to her next present. "A dictionary," she shrugged.

"Not exactly," said my mother, "It's a book of synonyms."

I was curious. I had just been studying synonyms at school during a unit on poetry. "Can I look?" I asked, and my sister handed me the book. In our house, Christmas always meant loads and loads of presents under the tree, so many in fact, that for a long time, the notion of Santa Claus offered the only reasonable explanation. Certainly my parents could never afford all these gifts! This year was no different.

Except this year, everything was different.

This year, I cared little about the presents. What I wanted could never be given, and the usual excitement of Christmas morning was replaced, for me, by a solemnity verging on apathy. The thesaurus caught my attention, and seemed to beckon, as if to say, "I can give you what you want." This, of course, was absurd. How could a book of words give me back my brother? How could all those synonyms have anything worthwhile to say about where he was now. How could anything, anything at all, make the pain and the missing go away.

My brother, Patrick Francis, was named after two saints, one who drove the snakes out of Ireland and the other who charmed wolves and wild creatures to his side. I used to think this was funny, a sort of contradiction inherent in his name, and I was curious to see what sort of person he would be as he grew older. But he was only eighteen months old when he was abruptly snatched from my life, and all I would remember was the quirky, restless character of the baby I adored.

He died because he had a hole in his heart. It was because of the hole that he was not strong enough to fight the pneumonia that took hold of his lungs during flu season that year. And when he became progressively weaker, they took him to the Children's Hospital in Denver, far away from our Colorado Springs home. The day before they took him, I sat in the rocker with him for many hours. My mother was sick in her bed, and Patrick, who was feverish and ill at ease himself, cried incessantly. The only time he was quiet was while I rocked him, and so I sat with him all through the day, talking softly, humming Brahms' Lullaby, and stroking his soft head. This was a thing I often did, to ease him to sleep or calm him when he cried. When I sang to him, he always settled right down. My family used to say I was the only one who had this effect upon him, and it was always me my mother called when she needed someone to hold him. "You have secret powers," my little sister Laura would say. Deep down, I thought this must be true.

After he died, I used to think that if only they had let him stay with me in the rocking chair, he would have been all right. It was like a spell that had been broken when they whisked him away, and on the third day in the hospital, the doctor told my parents to go home. There was no more they could do, he said; their baby would not make it through the night. It was hard to think about Patrick dying all alone in the hospital without anyone who loved him, and it made me feel as though there was a gaping hole in my own heart. If it had been me, I thought, I'd have wanted to die in my mother's arms. And if I could have held him when he took his last breath, that is what I would have done. So why, I wondered, didn't my mother? Why did she leave him there to die alone? The question tugged at the hole in my heart, and the empty space inside me grew.

I sat on the sofa and looked up the word "death" in the thesaurus. Next to it was the word *quietus*. I liked the sound of this word, and I sat pondering it. Did it really mean death, such a pleasant word, like a cool washcloth over a hot face in a darkened room. I looked it up, and it led me to *exit* which led to *gate*. It was marvelous to me, the way one word opened up to all others.

I kept going, looking up word after word, and to the sound of my mother cooking dinner in the kitchen, I made a poem. I titled my poem "Death Equals Birth":

Quietus is dark
Like my mother
when she goes into her room and
stays a long time,
hours or days
Stone cold quiet.
My mother's room is a dark cave
Where we are not allowed to go,
and there is no exit.
Maybe my mother has died
a thousand deaths in her room.
But there is a hidden gate
I know about; it is hidden
In her mouth. Her mouth
Is the gate, and in her belly,
Is a word
Waiting to get out.
It won't die, but it can't be born.

Death means quietus which means
decease, which means exit
which means gate
Which means opening,
which means beginning
Which means genesis which means
Birth.

If my mother would only speak the word,
  a whole world could be born
But She only cries.

It was interesting to me that when I wrote a poem about death, what came out was not about Patrick, but about my mother. My mother came to sit beside me now on the couch, and I hid the poem away in the book.

"Why are you crying?" she asked.

How could I tell her? We had never spoken about my brother's death. In my family not one word was ever said about it. Except at the funeral. But that was the priest who spoke. He told us our baby was in heaven now, with God, and that we could pray to Patrick and he would help us. He said God had "plucked" him, as one might a beautiful flower, and that God had done this because Patrick was so special and beautiful in His sight, He wanted him by His side.

I didn't believe a word he said, and now, in the shadow of my mother's question, I said, "God doesn't pluck little babies like a flower." I had meant to ask it as a question, but it came out as a statement. And so I added, "Does He?" My mother seemed surprised by my words, and she was quiet for a moment before she put her arm around me and pulled me closer. "I don't know," she said.

It was the first time my mother had sat with her arm around me since before Patrick died. I lay my head against her breast the way I'd once done, though I'd grown taller and everything seemed out of proportion now. After awhile, I broke the silence by saying, "Won't he ever come back?"

The question sounded so silly, I wished I'd never spoken. I tried to make it sound better by saying, "Maybe the doctors made a mistake. Maybe it was a different baby."

My mother turned away slightly, and I was ashamed for bringing it up. Her voice was flat when she said, "No, the doctors didn't make a mistake. He can't come back."

"But you weren't there. You left. You don't know for sure." I thought she might be mad at me for pushing the issue, but I kept going. I wanted to know.

"I wasn't there when he died, but I was with him constantly for three days before he died. I could see he would never wake up."

"But why did you leave him? Why didn't you hold him until the end? You left him." It was a thing I could never understand.

"I was sick," she said. "I'd got the flu and I was burning up with fever. I could hardly stand or even sit. My head was pounding and everything blurred around me. The doctor told me to go home, he said there was nothing more

I could do, that Patrick was dying. I said I would stay until the end, but your father picked me up and carried me to the car and I didn't have the strength or will to fight. I was crying that I wanted to stay, but none of them listened."

She reminded me that I had seen his body, in his casket at the funeral home the day before he was buried. "But it didn't look like him," I argued. "It wasn't even his clothes."

"I'd gone to the store and bought him special clothes to be buried in," said my mother. "And when the funeral director prepares a body for burial, it often makes the person look different. But it was him."

We sat there in silence for a little while, but before my mother got up from the couch, she handed me a gift. "I thought you should have one of your own," she said, and before I even opened it, I knew what it would be. It was the same size and shape of the book I held in my lap, and opening it, I felt, for the first time all day, a rush of excitement.

That night, our whole family gathered for games, as was our custom on Christmas night. During the Scrabble game, I made up sentences in my mind using words that had been played on the board. It was a thing I liked to do, to make things more interesting. Usually the sentences were silly ones like: *dogs die quickly*, or *frogs jump home*. But tonight the sentences seemed full of meaning: *you must dive deep, you must live well*, and then the most startling one of all: *you must use secret powers*. I wondered if the others saw what I saw, and if they did, did they understand its importance. I looked around the table, but they were all studying their letters with serious faces.

I took the sentences to be a message from my brother, and that night, when I thought everyone was asleep, I walked out to the living room where the lights of the Christmas tree gave a soft glow to the darkened room. I didn't notice my mother lying on the couch, and because I thought I was alone, I began to perform a ritual I had devised. I lit a candle, then stood with my hands over my heart. I was about to begin to sing, when my mother spoke to me and startled me out of my meditation. "What are you doing, Katy?"

I was taken off guard, embarrassed, and wasn't sure what to answer. The words slipped out of my mouth before I had time to censor them. "I'm using my secret powers to mend the hole in my heart."

I heard my mother breathe a deep sigh, and then, ever so gently that I felt all the strength go out of me, she asked, "Can I help?"

"Come here," she beckoned and I went to sit by her on the couch. She sat up and held me in her lap and she began to stroke my hair. It was such a tender thing, a thing she had not done in a very long time, and I could not hold back my tears. This was the first time I really cried about Patrick's death. I had wept at various times, but not like this. Now I sobbed, great convulsing, sobs while my mother rocked me slowly, back and forth . . . until, to the sound of her humming Brahms' Lullaby, I fell asleep in her arms.

Kate Fitzgerald is a freelance writer whose primary focus is fiction. She lives in the Driftless region of southwestern Wisconsin where, having raised four children, she now writes and edits from home. She has taught high school English and journalism, worked at her local bookstore, and contributed news and feature stories to the *Kickapoo Free Press*. She is currently writing a young adult novel. Email Kate at fitz.kate02@gmail.com.

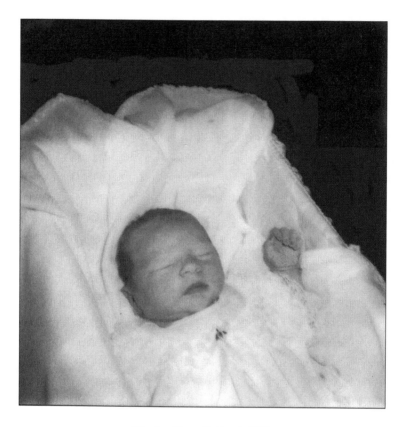

Heather Dawn Ecklund, 1976

*"A photo of my dear, older sister,
how could she not know that I needed to see it?"*

HEATHER DAWN

AManda Elderkin

Heather Dawn. I always loved her name. When I say it to myself, I see a sunrise on an Irish moor. Heather was my older sister. She had a huge influence on my life, but our relationship was quite unlike most.

I have never met Heather Dawn. At least in this lifetime. But I have felt her absence throughout my life. Sometimes more than others.

I have a distinct memory of being 8 or 9, and learning that my mother had always had a photo of Heather. From after she died. I felt so betrayed. How could she have kept this from me? A photo of my dear, older sister, how could she not know that I needed to see it? When I saw the photo, oh, there she was! Kind of gray, definitely without life, but I could see her body! This was the part I had been missing. And she was a redhead like me. No one had told me that. This detail made me feel even more connected to her, and somehow that made her being gone hurt even more.

Before and after that day, I cried myself to sleep at the loss of her most nights. As an adult looking back, I remember feeling the hole her absence left in my life so viscerally. With her gone I became the oldest. I suppose being raised Mormon, as a child I had a heightened sense of spirit and afterlife, but I don't feel like it was imagination that gave me this sense of loss.

At age 9, my grandma took me on my first plane ride. We went to Utah to see my aunt and uncle and their first baby. I loved the airplane. I was so excited. I had a Coke for my beverage on the flight. To this day, I associate the taste of Coke, which I didn't drink much, with sitting on that plane, next to Grandma in the recycled air, looking out at the high-sky views. During that week or so, I insisted that we visit Heather's grave. It felt so important. Like it would give me the something I was looking for whenever I felt her absence. I made sure we bought some flowers at a grocery store on our way to the cemetery. We walked over the spring grass, searching for her section. There was her little headstone.

All alone, among the other Mormon babies who had died, but nowhere near any other family members. She is the only family member of mine who died until my grandmothers passed when I was in my 20s. She is still in that plot, surrounded by strangers.

My visit to Heather's grave was short. It didn't satisfy the gap in my life, or explain why her death had affected me so much. I think I was hoping for a spiritual experience sitting with her earthy home that day. I remember wishing I could cry. To wail and wish her back, right there, like I did at night in my bed, but with the proof of her life right in front of me. I think I could've sat there until nightfall, but my relatives were ready to go, and my nine-year-old self didn't want to make a fuss over a relationship that didn't make any sense to anyone else.

In my 'tween years, I felt Heather's presence strongly. She was with me wherever I went. I listened to my intuition to sense her. I'd tell my friends, "Heather's sitting in that chair." Her presence helped calm me, but I do think I freaked out my friends on more than one occasion.

From what I can tell, Heather Dawn died from Respiratory Distress Syndrome, a complication of her being born at 35 weeks gestation. My parents were living in Provo, Utah, at the time, and my father was to be doing his Army Reserve training around her due date. Because of this, my mother's birth plan was to go back home to Wisconsin to give birth there and be supported by my grandmother. But Heather came early, was born in Provo, and died later that day in Salt Lake City.

What I know is that she was born healthy, and then plummeted. She was transported to a hospital with a higher tech nursery, but she didn't make it. The surfactant, a lubricant in the lungs that makes their inflation possible, hadn't developed yet. She just couldn't breathe. She died the day she was born. She was my parents' first baby. It was June 9, 1976.

I was born in August 1977. So you can see that I have never met Heather Dawn. And my grief for her passing is my own, as my parents were very comforted by their religion, and didn't have any noticeable suffering over her passing once I arrived. I remember growing up with the story that my parents rode in the funeral limo with her body, and that this was possible because of the small size of her coffin. My mom would say that she felt at peace with her loss after the funeral. Even recently, she told me that Heather's death didn't impact her labor with me: the second baby.

Now I am 34 years old, and a homebirth midwife. I deal with the doorway between life and death more than most do. And I do it without an ER or OR next door. I don't think of Heather as much as I used to, but sometimes when I tell people I am the eldest of six kids, or the eldest of 30-some grandchildren on my mom's side, I feel like I'm lying or cheating her of her spot in the lineup.

For a chunk of time in the past few years, I took a sabbatical and spent a few days a week being a nanny for a family that had gone through the loss of a baby. My primary responsibility was to care for the child who came after the baby who died. I felt a deep kinship with her. We both had the experience of being the forest that rose after the fallen tree. Our family structures are very different in several ways, but she will also grow up knowing her older sister without meeting her here.

We have had too many babies die in our community in the past few years. Some stillborn for unknown reasons, some who didn't make it through birth, some who couldn't survive the transition to extra-uterine life. Yesterday I was at a birth where life and death were both in the room. Life won this time. I. Am. So. Grateful. Recently I have been looking to Heather, the baby who died, for some perspective in this role of incredible responsibility I have chosen.

After that birth yesterday, I am questioning my personal need to work in a field so intense, and so unsupported by the medical and legal systems. I can be a guardian of normal birth, and do my job well, and babies can still die. Babies die everyday in the hospital. The United States' infant mortality rate is #34 in the world, according to the United Nations list. Almost every European country beats us over and over again in this assessment. In Europe, midwives are an integral part of care in the childbearing year, and homebirth is a normal option. For example, in the Netherlands, which ranks #18, 34 percent of women give birth at home. Our homebirth rate just went from 1 percent to 2 percent. As a midwife, I am actually part of the solution, not the problem. As a surviving family member, I know something about what is at stake.

Birth is like life. It's risky. We can only do so much to maintain control. If Heather had had the steroids that are routinely given nowadays to mothers showing signs of preterm labor, her lungs would've developed. She would've breathed. She would've lived. She would've taken care of me. I wouldn't have had to be the oldest, with all the responsibilities that came with in my family. Should I blame technology? Should I blame the care my mother and unborn sister received? Honestly, I don't know enough of the details to judge the care that was given. This is where being the second baby and the adult midwife meet.

Being a midwife is like mothering. It's the hardest job you'll ever love. I know that death happens. I know that sometimes you can't do anything to stop it from coming. And many times, in my line of work, I can. But we Americans are so afraid of death that we just attack and sue others for not keeping it away. So now I (and dare I say that most midwives I know do this on a regular basis) question my personal need to BE the birth revolution.

I am no longer Mormon. As an adult, I have always been someone who finds power and solace in the spirituality of our earth. When I am driving to a birth, I pray to deities and ancestors. I call on Heather, the baby who died, to assist me and help me be present, aware, listen to my intuition, and make smart decisions.

Death comes, and all we can do is learn from it. Be with the pain of life, and the fecundity of what grows out of it. Maybe this perspective comes from my earliest loss: the death that happened before I was born. I don't claim to be an expert on anything but my own experience, but I am grateful that this deep knowing tempers my recurring question of career choice. Maybe it's why I can stand at the gate of life, where death lingers, and be okay.

AMANDA ELDERKIN, LM, CPM, is a homebirth midwife in private practice and employed at a local birth center. She graduated from the National

Midwifery Institute and did her hands-on training with a local homebirth practice and at a high-volume birth center on the border of Texas and Mexico. She loves writing, painting, music, ritual, and family. She has published her paintings a few times, but this is her first published writing. She lives in Northern California with her partner and two daughters. www.amandaelderkin.net

Eric Stull, M.D. and his wife, Kyoko Katayama

Let everything happen to you: beauty and terror.
Just keep going. No feeling is final.
Don't let yourself lose me.
                                        Rainer Maria Rilke

ONE DAY I WILL
BREATHE HIM

Kyoko Katayama

I had decided to take a trip to visit my old and dear friends in Florence, Italy. Something compelled me to go there where I used to live in the '70s. I wanted to see their sparkling eyes surrounded by the small rivulets of wrinkles. I wanted to touch their rough, dirt-stained hands. I wanted to get lost in the olive groves, their terrain.

I was approaching the 12th month of mourning since my beloved husband Eric died. I felt stunned that nearly a year passed. It was like yesterday, it was like another lifetime.

Time has been such a weird, crazy, intriguing reflection of my states, like the crazy mirrors at the state fair. I remembered my meditation teacher telling me years ago that time does not exist outside of our mind. It is an illusion. I have been living that illusive time. It has made me both scream with the pain of never being able to see him and touch him again, and smile with the tender knowing of love all around me. How have I held these extreme experiences, of a blade in the heart and the salve of love, and everything in between.

This has been a strange time in other ways, too. The forsythia bloomed six weeks early this spring. A year ago, as Eric slowly exhaled for the last time, tiny yellow petals of forsythia quietly blossomed outside his window. I am so used to gauging my rhythm with that of the trees, flowers, birds, and animals around us, and when they were out of season, at least the seasons I knew, I felt ungrounded. Something felt off. But then, everything was "off" this past year. I've stared into the crazy mirror, tear-smeared, confused, overwhelmed. The mirror asked back: Who are you without Eric?

When Eric died, I felt that a part of me died, too, but I did not know what part. I thought grieving was about missing him and crying. The experience of the loss was nothing like I imagined. Death is a mystery. Too, the mystery of being left alive. What do they all mean?

One of my "grieving" tasks became to learn to re-embrace my aliveness when death and the end of myriad things loomed so large, not just outside of me but deep inside of me. As Eric's organs were slowly disintegrating, my being was taking in the truth of the predicament that everything that is born must also die. In my animal body, the cells understood impermanence. Everything that arises also passes away, the Buddha said. My mind must catch up with these profound truths, the gift of his death, and at the same time I have had the difficult task of not losing sight of the evidences of my own aliveness.

In Florence, I hoped to experience and witness my aliveness and that of others in the safety of my welcoming friends, whose old stone house was tucked in the middle of the olive groves. I wanted to pay attention to how this aliveness might manifest in the details of my everyday life. The travel to Florence was a much wished-for trip that Eric couldn't make. My friends there planted a young cypress tree in his memory soon after he died. I packed a small portion of Eric's ashes to bury under that tree.

It had been sunny and warm there, my friends told me on Skype, but the forecast showed that the weather would turn cold and wet just in time for my arrival! My heart sank. I was leaving the unseasonably warm, dry, about-to-bloom Minnesota for wet, cold, Tuscan hills. Well, here is your opportunity, I told myself, see if you can feel your stupendous, priceless, most precious aliveness when the rain pours down on you in the midst of a misty old olive grove!

I flew to Florence via Amsterdam. The plane pierced through the night sky like a bullet toward north. How strange it was to be alive, holding his ashes 30,000 miles above ground. I dozed as I considered that neither Eric nor I was quite on Earth at the moment. When I awoke, I saw strange light out of the window. It looked like giant brushstrokes of light against the black backdrop. In a few minutes, they changed into curtains of light. They shimmered across the sky beneath the sharp, waxing moon and the studs of stars. When my eyes got used to the dark, I could make out below the vast, snow-covered landmass receiving the moonlight in shades of blue. Perhaps we were above Iceland. The sight was out of this world, another planet. My forehead against the cool glass pane, I peeked and peeked until my neck ached and tiny oval window became steamy. I couldn't believe my luck, the luck of being alive and seeing this magic show of light.

We buried the ashes on Easter Sunday, my friends and I. The baby cypress stood green and straight, at the edge of their olive grove, surrounded by blooming tulips.

The sky was dark grey and raining, but beneath the misty grove, the ground eagerly drank the rain after many months of drought, and the trees around us pushed up their verdant branches and leaves towards the sky. They shouted, "Rain, rain, come down on us!" and fluttered and shimmered their thousands of tiny hands in joy.

Stefano dug a small hole at the foot of the cypress. My friends had planted a bunch of tulips so the tree wouldn't be lonely. The sight was tender and full of the hope of spring, such contrast to the small bundle of Eric's ashes—actually crushed bones—wrapped in paper. I took it out from a heart-shaped box and placed it in the hole. We took turns covering it with the wet earth. The ashes would soon be completely soaked, dissolving among the roots of the young cypress and the orange and red tulips.

The earth was acidic yellow ocher. His ashes and bones will balance the acidity, and together with the rain and the sun, they will nourish the tree. It will grow tall and poke the sky, emitting oxygen, and the air will travel around the world. One day I will breathe in that air. "And you will hear the air itself, like a beloved, whisper: oh, let me, for a while longer, enter the two beautiful bodies of your lungs," Mary Oliver wrote.

From the corner of their shed, Stefano carried a big marble stone that they had found with Nina, our eldest daughter, when she was a little girl. He bent down to place it over the fresh earth. Janet put her hand on his back. I felt held by their care. Then we stood in silence surrounding the tree, in simplicity and completion.

Now it is the night before Eric's first anniversary. A year ago tonight I slept on the couch near his bed. He rang the little bell by his bed to wake me and asked for some water. His inside was burning from so much vomiting, and he was so dehydrated. In a day, he would be gone . . . oh, **basta**! as they say in Italy. Enough. I want to remember the sound of his laughter; I want to remember him in the height of his vitality. Remember the thousand ways of his kindness and his generosity. He is free from suffering now, and I want to remember him in ways that I, too, will be free.

I took on the task of asking myself what makes me feel alive every day. What died in me when he died? I went to Italy with these questions. Lately I thought if I were a Christian, I would answer: I feel most alive when I am close to God. But for me, I need a different language than God. I realized that I was asking a very big question by asking the question of aliveness, as big and as central as the question of God. I felt alive when I felt joy in working together in the olive field with my friends. But, too, I felt alive crying hard, sitting on a bench overlooking the hills. When I lifted my tear-stung face, the misty hills with myriad shades of springing greens spread as far as the eyes could see, and the cry turned into a gasp for the beauty. The three of us, the Grief, the Gratitude, and I, sat side by side on that bench, speechless and stunned. We were held somehow. What grace it was.

All I know tonight is that I need to keep on asking the question. Perhaps I will have a different answer everyday, but it doesn't matter. This is one question where asking is an answer.

One metaphor for losing Eric is that it is like losing a limb. I thought about all the new ways I would have to figure out how to be in the world if I lose, let's say, my right arm. So I pretended that I didn't have a right arm, and I tried to do things with my left arm for a time being. Since I was writing when I thought of this, I switched to write with my left hand. I could hardly make letters out. It went slowly and awkwardly, not able to keep up with what I wanted to write. I thought about 60 years of training my right hand to do things while my left hand idly watched the right hand do its work. Without the right hand, the left hand would have to develop new muscles and new habits. My brain would have to grow a gazillion new neurons in the meantime. But it is not impossible for my left hand to learn to do things, if given time and practice. I was sure of it. It dawned on me that if I lost a limb, my task would be to remember and call on all the parts of the body I still have.

I was awake at 3 a.m. last night and couldn't get back to sleep. After a fretting hour, I decided to do the body scan meditation. I focused on the sensations of my little toes, then the soles of the feet, the heels, the ankles, shins . . . limb by limb, organ by organ . . . I felt the beautiful symmetry of my limbs, the vitality of my lungs and heart, and the quiet, reassuring work of the liver and the kidneys, the bloodstreams and the interstitial fluid . . . I fell asleep feeling whole and strong.

So this morning, I remember Eric, the ways he was alive and well. His smile, the twinkle in his blue-green eyes, how he used to put his right hand on his heart when he talked about things that mattered. I put my hand over my heart and say, "Eric, I love you. Love is eternal, and you and I are part of the unending circle."

Kyoko Katayama's poetry has been published in the *Asian American Renaissance Journal* and an anthology, *Intersecting Circles: The Voices of Hapa Women in Poetry and Prose*. She was a recipient of a scholarship for Inroads, a program for emerging Asian/Pacific Islander writers sponsored by the Loft Literary Center in Minneapolis. Currently she is working on a memoir about the death of her beloved husband and her first year without him. She lives in St. Paul, Minnesota, with her dog, Luna, who now occupies the spot in the bed where her husband used to sleep.

The O'Donnell family camping in the Cascade River State Park in northern Minnesota in 1996.
Steve, Doreen, Katie, Joe in stripes, Dan at the bottom.

"You left when Joey was just five. He doesn't remember you,
except the memories he conjures up from the photos I took."

Twenty-five Years
of Love Lessons
Doreen O'Donnell

H appy Anniversary, BABY, got you on my—MI-IND . . . .
Hi Steve, today is January 7, our twenty-fifth wedding anniversary. At
least, it would be, if you were still here. You died twelve years ago. Wow. You've
been gone from my life almost as long as you were in it.

You left when Joey was just five. He doesn't remember you, except the
memories he conjures up from the photos I took. He is the one who looks like
you, from his freckly face down to his skinny, white legs. He loves that about
himself.

Danny was nine. I asked if it bothered him to be raised in a one-parent
family. He said, "Mom, most of my friends are in one-parent families." His glib
one-liners are the bones he throws so no one will discover the pain he has
carried since you disappeared from his life.

Katie was eleven. You were her Knight in Shining Armor. She became very
angry.

I was thirty-seven the day I learned your plane went down, the day the
village cop came to my door, fax in hand from an office in New Mexico, half
a country away. That flight would be the last time your will would overrule
mine. Before you left, just two days earlier you gave me a passionate good-bye,
so happy you were off on this great adventure with your friend, Bill. Finally
you were doing something that didn't involve work, that was just plain fun.
You called that night to let me know you had arrived safely, and would be
returning the next day in your newly purchased airplane. I said a somewhat
unwilling, "I love you." You knew I didn't want you to buy that plane. We never
spoke again.

Now I am a year older than you were when you died.

Twenty-five years. The first thirteen were with you. What did I learn during that time? I learned how to haul water and to split wood with a maul, and that ashes work great on icy driveways. I learned how to make maple syrup. I learned how to stand my ground (even though you're OLDER than I am, it doesn't mean you know EVERYTHING!). I learned how to laugh. I learned how to have a baby, how to rock a baby, how to nurse a baby, how to read to one child while nursing another, and how to hold those children close while I mourned the loss of twin boys.

I learned how to plow snow. I learned how to grow and can nearly all of the fruit and vegetables that we ate. I learned that I am a very good teacher. I learned how to be the administrator of our little woodworking business, so you could do the hands-on stuff, and how to hold down the fort while you were off doing important political work.

Then one day, I learned what it feels like to find out that you died. Really, it felt like nothing. Blank. You were here, now you were gone.

The following twelve years have been very different. Lesson number one was how to open my eyes that first morning, look at the children in bed with me, and realize that the previous night really happened. The policeman did come to the door and, as if by magic, the house did fill up with friends. I also learned, or maybe knew all along, that I had to keep some semblance of order, to remain calm so the children would not feel afraid.

That's pretty much been the undertone, except for the time that I decided I deserved to have what I thought I wanted, temporarily putting the children on hold. I decided to see what it would be like to have a new love. I told myself that he would be good for the children. They didn't like him, and eventually I realized I didn't, either. By that time, though, the children didn't view me the way they used to. It took years before they knew they could trust me again. I learned the hard way that putting myself before the children was a bad idea.

I learned how to be a runner. I ran competitively for several years, with medals to prove it. I think that would surprise you. You know I never was athletic. I also put my little toe into politics, and was town clerk for two terms. That would surprise you, too, since I always stayed in the background while you were here. I learned how to use a chainsaw.

I learned that I could survive Katie, whose anger was so fierce, I often wondered if she wished I'd died instead of you. I asked her about that recently.

That wasn't it. She just missed you so much, and she didn't know what to do with that. So we were all miserable for, oh, about seven years. But you should see her now! She is married to a fine man who has softened her hard edges, and she is a straight-A student at the University of New Mexico.

Dan and Joe are as tall as you were, and it looks as though they are still growing. Dan studied his way to Dartmouth College, and he has found his niche there. Joe will graduate second in his high school class this spring. I've learned that our decision to educate our children at home for as long as we could, to focus on their education, wherever they received it, was the right one. You were in there with me on that. In fact, it was your idea. I second-guessed myself a lot. I wondered if we were making a mistake. That is my favorite thing I've learned—that following my gut, focusing on my family instead of myself, was a great choice. Being a mom is the best career I ever could have chosen.

My dad's death last year prompted something that I had put on hold while I was raising our children. I hadn't fully grieved for you. I didn't have time to be alone, to think, to feel. The grief literature I have read refers to it as a kind of unresolved grief, called delayed grief. The time had come. I spent the months following my dad's death holding my breath while in public and was almost immobile when I was home alone. I took the phone off the hook. I declined invitations to dinner with friends. I protected what I now realized was something I never had—time to grieve your death. During that time I learned that I am not angry with you anymore, that I really, really miss you. One more thing—I learned that I wouldn't be who I am if you hadn't been in my life. And that was a very good lesson to learn.

Doreen O'Donnell has had articles and poems published in the *Wisconsin Poets Calendar, the Green Bay Press Gazette,* and the *Kickapoo Free Press.* She lives in the woods of southwestern Wisconsin on her registered tree farm and works as a secretary for Vernon Memorial Health Care Home Care and Hospice in Viroqua, Wisconsin. Doreen can be reached at odonnell.doreen@yahoo.com.

Kristen Savitri Bergh

"The journey was messy and uneven, but I find now that from the beginning, the possibility of healing my soul, of finding a future, and of keeping a connection to my beloved Kirsten were always present."

FINDING THE WAY FORWARD

LINDA BERGH

My husband Paul, 54, died unexpectedly after a cardiac arrest related to an enlarged heart in August 1995. A year later, our only child Kirsten, age 17, decided to attend a school a thousand miles from our home in Minnesota. She and her best friend Nina started school at a Waldorf High School in upstate New York.

On November 28, 1996, Thanksgiving Day, I arrived in Harlemville, New York, to visit Kirsten. Due to a late plane, we spent only a few hours together on Thanksgiving night. We cuddled for a long time, not wanting to leave each other, she especially. We finally said goodnight.

Early the next morning on a trip to a thrift store, our car slid on black ice across the midline and smashed into a 16-wheel truck. Kirsten and Nina died instantly. I was alive but severely mangled. After the car was pried open with jaws, I was airlifted to the local hospital to undergo a 14-hour surgery, my facial bones shattered, my eye pierced, and many bones broken. I was in ICU while a three-day vigil and a funeral were held in the community where the Kirsten and Nina were going to school. One week later I was medically flown to Minneapolis, to try to save my eye. I was in the hospital for six weeks with my jaw wired shut. Having lost one eye, I went home, fragile and homebound, facing my losses.

It is now 15 years later, and I am exploring the question of how I healed from these losses. Many people over the years have asked me how I moved back into life after the loss of Kirsten. For this article, I decided to look back at the first journal entries after the accident. In them, I find the seeds of transformation in the dark earth of those early days. It is stunning to me, even now, that a voice of hope and of future threaded through. The journey was messy and uneven, but I find now that from the beginning, the possibility of healing my soul, of finding a future, and of keeping a connection to my beloved Kirsten were always present. I share these journal entries in that light.

In March 1997, dear friends who stayed with me in my ICU room in the hospital in New York take me with them to the warmth of Mexico. My hand and arm have been in a cast for six weeks. It is here, three months after the accident, that I start to write in my journal.

> *I feel unearthly, invisible.*
>
> *Oh, Kirsten, I keep seeing things through your eyes—I want to share everything with you. I had promised to bring you to Mexico.*
>
> *Every minute I miss you so, I can hardly hold the feeling.*
>
> *I try to write what happened. It is soul splitting. Even now it sears my heart to write the words. "I saw a huge truck coming toward us, and we were crossing the midline . . ." Every night in the hospital I had this vision. I would see it all in red, and then try to change it, to avoid the accident, to bring you back.*
>
> *Why do I write? To not forget you. But how could I forget you? Every action of every day was for you. Wanting to give you the opportunity to live a life as free from prejudice as possible and as full of self-love as possible. Your young life surpassed any ideas I had about how free and vital and clear someone could be. You had already become my teacher, my inspiration. So what do I do now without you?*
>
> *I long to share this Earth with you, and letting you go is the hardest thing I have ever done. I don't know how to find the you in me. I feel numb and invisible and have no idea what will bring me to life again. But I ask you to be on this journey with me. Help me open to the love of spirit within me. Help me to find a new life.*

What would I say to you if I were on the other side and you were here? I'd tell you to live deeply and fully in your life, to not hold back; to tell the truth as you see it; to respect others and yourself; to move through fear to fulfillment.

When I think of you and feel flutterings that make me shiver, is that your answer, or my own? Is my grief okay with you? It comes in spurts and blobs. I miss you. I remember you. Where did all the aliveness go? How can I find answers? Are there things you want me to work on down here on Earth for you? Help me to know what they are.

Dream: being with Kirsten and friends, hanging out together. Enjoying each other, laughing. Lightheartedness. Joy. I want to stay in this dream.

My body aches I miss you so much.

The clock stopped. Everything looks different. I don't know who I am. Caught in a net, I look out into a world where I do not belong. Who is my life for? How do I move into a new perspective with the people I supported gone from my life? For countless centuries, women have lost their children; it is humanity's most ancient, inevitable sorrow. I am not alone.

I think of your love, and my body instantly fills with a flood of love and shivers. Can we seek joy, or does it come to us on our own? I can at least have the intention. The other night I was able to dance for a few minutes. For those moments, I felt "myself." I felt your spirit with me, smiling.

I am filled with a feeling of you as I stare at the slim sliver of light alone in the night sky. Peace and comfort wash over my loss. I feel related to that sliver of light as though connected by a thread. We mothers want our children, if only by a thread. So now the moon is my thread. I stare at your picture and I cry. Oh sweet moon, grant me your serenity as I walk the lonely road to my future. I know not who I am without the loves of my life. Sweet curve of crescent moon, carry me to see Kirsten when I sleep tonight.

The next entries were written after I returned home to Minnesota in mid-March. A friend helped me put together Kirsten's poetry and art into a book, *She Would Draw Flowers*, which was given out at her memorial service in April. I went through another surgery in May when a metal bar screwed to my facial bones protruded into my mouth.

March 14:

Today life looks too big. Too overwhelming. I don't want to do anything. The sky has opened up and sucked them away. I am spinning. I am directionless. What have I done with my life? What has it been for? My house is dark and cluttered.

Get out of this inner space. Don't give it credence. I am worthy, loving, light-filled, loved. I will heal. I will find a new direction. It is coming toward me. I must be patient and listen. I will find my way.

March 26:

I found pictures of Kirsten's birth and early life. Overwhelming. So much love, so much life. It brings such a profound loss of the physical. Help me hang on. I will light the candle, say the verse, send her and Paul my embrace to join them on their journey.

March 27: *I dream I am in Kirsten's room. There is a live bluebird, very tiny. Kirsten puts the bird in her hands and lets it eat. She is so loving and compassionate. I awake happy. Bluebird of happiness. Building a new soul life. Thank you for this dream.*

Easter: Lake Superior with dear friends: I awake knowing stronger than ever that she lives on, though my tears flow profusely in my missing. I long to hold her in my arms, to hear her raucous laugh, to see her awe and wonder at the deer that crossed the yard at dawn. I spin to years ahead. Oh, Kirsten, I miss already your mothering and my grandmothering. The future stretches endlessly like the ice across Lake Superior, only I cannot see the other shore. I feel so utterly alone. I must be patient and let the shoreline find me.

April 4:

Kirsten's memorial: 400 candles held aloft in a room so filled with love it is visible. Kirsten's spirit is celebrated and felt in that space, healing us all. The presence of her loved ones brings her near to help us close her Earthly life and open to new ways of finding her. And everyone goes away with her book, a tribute to her open, loving spirit.

I am grateful to have drawn you into my womb, to have had the privilege of mothering you and guiding you, until you found yourself and could begin to guide us all. How did you get so wise? I miss you so much, but I am so grateful to have known you.

April 24:

Is it time for hope to palpably enter our lives? I don't know what it will look like. Will the sky look blue again? Will I hear the birds again? Laugh again at silly jokes? I have lost my family, my spouse, my child. I can't work. And I have a strange body. Where am I going? I truly don't have a clue. Sadness hovers behind my eyes.

May 2:

I feel like I'm looking through Kirsten's eyes and body. When I first saw the blackbird sitting on a nest in the alcove by our front door, I waved my arms and jumped up and down; then realized I was making motions just like Kirsten used to make. When I look at the blue wildflowers in the yard, tiny and delicate, I feel joy and excitement, just like Kirsten expressed each spring. Is this joy I feel my Kirsten?

To never see her again. Not for graduation or college or travels or coffee or boyfriends or babies or career choice or snuggling or music making or dancing or proud mama moments. I want her outside me. I don't know how to have her inside me. And if I do, it is to find my life? I want to go to Africa for her. Write good poetry or draw to lengthen the myth that she is still here. Oh, God, I miss her. Kirsten I miss you. But I will find joy again as well as grief. I will laugh with abandon again. Help me.

May 13:

It's jutting into my mouth, a metal bar. Fears, of piercing, of surgery, of problems, I collapse in tears. I go downstairs. I need to be held. I go to find my beloved friends who are my housemates. The tears today are for me, for the ongoing agony of a body that isn't all mine, that doesn't work, that constantly reminds me of my losses.

May 20:

What makes me get up every day? People ask me this. If it isn't my family, or my work, what is it? Is it to see the hibiscus blooming on my kitchen counter, or to talk to my goddaughter on the phone? Is it a force of life that supersedes comprehension—a hope that the future will come toward me?

In June, I return to Harlemville, New York, the community where Kirsten and Nina were attending school when they died. I am still very fragile but feel compelled to return. Nina's parents return for Nina's graduation, and together we plant trees in her and Kirsten's memory. This section includes a letter to Kirsten's classmates.

June 2:

This is Kirsten's path. I melted when I saw the hill behind the school and felt her presence—felt her everywhere, in the stones, in the school building, the memories flooding back of walking here with her. [I had visited the school with her in the summer.] For nine months every day in my mind, I have been picturing Kirsten in this place. And now I'm in the picture, but she is not here.

June 10:

To her classmates:

To walk the hill has been to walk with Kirsten. I can almost see her sneak a smile, write a note, give a hug, share a snack, make a joke. It has been a bittersweet time, for along with the joy of seeing all of you who she shared her brief time with here, I have waves of sadness for her not being here to sing and laugh and care about life. How do we go on from such a loss? How do we get up each day with meaning and enthusiasm when sadness wants to swallow us?

I don't pretend to have an answer. I think one thing we can all agree from knowing Kirsten. The lesson is not to pull back from life but to keep stepping forward to embrace it.

I want to say to all of you: take the risk to share your pain and joy with your friends. For what else can rebuild our trust in life? It takes courage to not bury our feelings. As I have reached out through this loss, and so many have reached to me, we find new threads of beginnings. We find those who can listen and who can hold our hearts. You will have Kirsten and Nina close to your hearts for your whole lives. And for that incomprehensible linkage, I am grateful.

What is this voice of hope and connection? In the hospital, words came to me clearly and simply without my asking in the phrase "Love is greater than fear." I am told that I repeated it to all who came to see me. I think it was not a personal voice, but a kind of knowing that held me during those immeasurable first days of loss. Then, when I went home from the hospital and began to face life again, it got messier. I had to find that voice again from a deeply personal, grieving place. In these journal entries of the first six months, that voice is as thin as gossamer thread, almost as invisible as I felt. But it was present, persevering and quietly helping me to reconstruct a loving world without my beloveds.

Somewhere in this process of healing, the accident shifted from something that happened to me to an event that happened. As the voice of connection and hope got stronger, I could slowly see my daughter's destiny as separate from mine and allow myself to be a grieving mother and a person who could feel happiness and connection in my life.

But make no mistake. It is not a simple journey. I keep learning that grief does not end; it keeps asking to be transformed. Just a year ago I had a disturbing dream, where Kirsten was a young teenager visiting at a friend's house, and I was waiting for her to come to the phone. I waited . . . and waited . . . and waited. She never came to the phone, and I awoke feeling totally disconnected. I could not reach her. I went into a place of raw grief I had not felt for a decade.

Realizing I was being stretched again, I had to further release my identity with the accident and with Kirsten. Seeing it instead as one event in my whole life, I chose again to live my life now, knowing that freedom and love, not fear, is what truly connects me to Kirsten. Something shifted.

Within days, an opportunity opened to do service at an orphanage in Thailand. So as the mother who had lost her daughter, I could go and be with children who had lost their parents. It lit my heart in a new way. I had a purpose toward the future. How can we know what continued healing and expansion will come from incomprehensible losses when we open our hearts?

Through meeting my life fully, Kirsten's spirit is truly still alive and well.

LINDA BERGH, psychologist emeritus and teacher, faced the loss of her only daughter and two husbands. She published her daughter's poetry, *She Would Draw Flowers,* and teaches courses for young people. She helped create the documentary *The Most Excellent Dying of Theodore Jack Heckelman.* She is a Midwest leader in the Conscious Dying/Home Death Care movement, available as a guide for families. One great passion is teaching biography locally, regionally, and internationally. She is fed by the beauty in nature, the wonder of children, and the joy of singing and dancing. Lifetime careers in teaching from Waldorf kindergarten to private college and therapy for children and families. www.beholdingthethreshold.org or find her on Facebook.

Caroline Kirk with her mother, Alison Kirk

*"Caroline helped us see the value of simply being present
in the moment with another soul. Our presence was the only gift
we could give her at the end of her life.*

SIMPLE PRESENCE

ALLISON KIRK

I have a video clip of my daughter Caroline, age four, sitting in her red wagon. She stares at the camera with a small smile on her face and says, "Don't forget, Alison." She was in that phase children go through of discovering that their parents have names beyond Mama and Daddy, and trying them out in a very adult fashion. I don't know what Caroline was referring to with "Don't forget" at the time she said it, but now the admonition resonates strongly within me. How could I ever forget my child? Caroline's life, and then her death, only changed the world for me.

Much of the trajectory of Caroline's life was determined in the womb. Her genetic disease ordained that her life would be short. The neurological progression of her disorder robbed her of physical and mental capacities as the years went by. We, as parents, were robbed of the hopes and dreams parents have for their children. I used to catalog all of the experiences Caroline would never have, all of the things she would never learn to do. It was exhausting. The sadness in her story is easy to find, but to look only at that aspect of Caroline's life is to shortchange her. The more difficult, and rewarding effort is finding and holding that which was completely right and good for Caroline. She lived the life she had. Her life was filled with play and learning while she was able, and then with being with the people who loved her. It was a complete life, and her legacy to us is the ability to view her life as complete. As enough. Her legacy is to be done once and for all with asking why, a question which has no answer to ease my heart.

When you look back at a life, it is tempting to do so in terms of accomplishments. The person went to this school, held this job, had so many children, won these awards, traveled to these countries. There would be no place in Caroline's obituary for a list of accomplishments. What could this quiet life of only nine years mean? The peculiar nature of her disease meant there would be no deathbed conversations, no last words to remember. We could not even fully explain to Caroline what was happening to her. We provided all the physical care of feeding and positioning and changing and bathing, managing oxygen and medications and suction. We read books, we sang songs, we described the world outside the window.

Most of the time, we simply were. Caroline helped us see the value of simply being present in the moment with another soul. Our presence was the only gift we could give her at the end of her life. When we could do nothing else for her, we could be present with our hearts open to her. Perhaps that is the only gift we can always give to another person. To be present and fully acknowledge that we have no answers, no solutions, that our community is all we have to offer at others' heartbreaking moments, is a challenge. It is tempting to say "It'll be okay," and proceed to rationalize our way through to that conclusion. It's hard not to try for a feel-good wrap-up. When people tell me, "It'll be okay," I often think "Or maybe it won't." This is not pessimism—this is realism. The gift I have come to value the most is the quiet reassurance that others will face with me what cannot be changed. That they will allow themselves to bear witness to the pain, and the rewards, in journeys such as ours with Caroline.

Caroline taught me to spend my heart, not holding back in fear of the separation we would undergo. She taught me that we are guaranteed nothing beyond this moment. Tolstoy wrote that now is the only time over which we have dominion. I felt the greatest connection with Caroline when I allowed myself to be fully present in the now with her. To do so was to be wholly cognizant of her illness, of her increasing frailty, as this was her experience. It is not easy to acknowledge that the days to come are fewer than those past, but the days become much more precious with this truth in mind.

Caroline had no belief that the world owed her anything. As I said, she lived the life she had. She became only more of who she truly was as she lost her concern with the trivial aspects of life. It was as though all of the nonessential elements of being were stripped away from her, and in what remained, there was no trace of resentment or anger. How could I be angry about her fate when she was so peaceful and accepting? Her peace was one that could be felt, and it was infectious. People fell in love with Caroline long after she ceased to make funny remarks or engage in games or share a piece of cake. They fell in love with her when she could do little more than gaze at them with her clear, peaceful eyes. I watched this happen and marveled at the impact my still, silent daughter had on others. I believe she reminded people of the beauty of existence, the beauty available in being present in each small moment. She invited people to participate in an ultimately uncomplicated love.

The world without Caroline is a sad place for me. A world in which Caroline has no relevance is an unbearable place for me. She can have meaning in this world as long as I carry her with me, as long as I consciously allow her memory to infuse me and influence my interactions. To continually ask why her life took the course it did is a question that promotes bitterness. To continually ask what did her life mean is a question that opens the heart. Caroline reminds me that there is value in holding a hand, in sharing a burden simply by showing up. She illustrates the importance of being aware in this moment, and that every moment is a gift.

ALISON KIRK lives in Nashville, Tennessee, where she worked as a clinical psychologist for many years. She and her husband Doug have two daughters with Niemann-Pick Disease type A/B: Caroline, who died in 2007, and Kate, age 11. To learn more about this disease and efforts to find a treatment/cure for it, please visit the website of the National Niemann-Pick Disease Foundation at nnpdf.org.

Diane Manahan and Nancy Manahan

The following two stories are excerpts from *Living Consciously, Dying Gracefully: A Journey with Cancer and Beyond* which recounts the extraordinary death of Diane Manahan, RN, MS, a professor of nursing at Minnesota State University, Mankato. Her husband Bill Manahan, MD, a holistic physician, had helped his wife to be in the driver's seat for her five-year journey with breast cancer. Then he, their four sons, their wives and a large circle of friends supported Diane to die at home, as she wished.

As part of the family's round-the-clock vigil, Bill slept with Diane as he had for the 37 years of their marriage, holding and comforting her when she would wake during the night and ask, "Why can't I die, Bill? I'm ready to go. Dying is harder than I thought it would be."

On the last morning of her life, Diane sat up while two of her grandchildren sang to her. Her sister-in-law, Nancy Manahan, took the next shift. No one realized it would be the last shift.

Two hours later, surrounded by her family, with Bill holding her hand, Diane Manahan slipped away, as consciously and as gracefully as she had lived her life. Nancy tells the story of Diane's last hours.

HOME FREE

NANCY MANAHAN

I could hardly grasp the reality: Diane, my beloved sister-in-law, was dying. This strong, healthy marathon runner had gone from hiking to walking to needing a cane to using a wheelchair. This popular college professor and gifted public speaker now whispered. She had lost almost 30 pounds, was profoundly jaundiced, had difficulty breathing, and hurt. Recently, while hugging her goodbye, I had inadvertently pressed on a tumor near her spine, and she had winced.

But the worst symptom, Diane said, was the unrelenting itching. Two weeks before, I had offered to give her a massage, which normally she would have loved. But this time she had asked for a body scratch.

Diane lay on the sofa, her supple, tan legs across my lap. While I was scratching her calves and thighs, Diane said she loved the poem I had sent her, Mary Oliver's "In Blackwater Woods." She asked me if I would read it at her Life Celebration. I said I would be honored. (She had asked many people to actively participate in this meticulously planned event.) We talked about it calmly, rationally, as if discussing her funeral were the most natural thing in the world.

On the 90-minute drive back home to Minneapolis, I gripped the steering wheel, sobbing, gasping, and howling as wave after wave of grief washed through me. How could I let her go?

Ten days later, on July 13, 2001, I returned to southern Minnesota. When I arrived in Mankato, my brother told me, "Diane's ready to die, but she doesn't know how to do it. She's so strong she could live for several days or even weeks."

Diane was lying in bed, looking tired but beautiful. There were no visible signs of cancer. Their daughter-in-law Kate later told me that two days earlier, after she had given Diane a bath, Diane's stylist had come to the house to wash and style her hair. As I leaned over to kiss her hello and hold her hand, I could smell her fresh, warm scent.

"Diane, it's Nancy. I know it's late, but I wanted to say hello."

She nodded and squeezed my hand. I sat on the bed and tried to be an open channel for comfort and peace, letting loving energy flow toward Diane.

Bill knew I had to leave soon. After a few minutes, he moved to the bed and bent over. Diane put her arms around his neck, and he helped her stand up and walk to the bathroom. She sat unsupported on the toilet.

"Goodnight, Sweetie," I said from the bathroom doorway. "I'll be back in the morning."

"Okay," Diane whispered, a smile barely lifting the corners of her mouth.

Diane's sister Patt stayed until ten o'clock that evening. She told me that before she left, she leaned over the bed and said, "Good night, Diane. I love you." Diane whispered back, "I love you, too." Those were the last words she ever spoke.

Topher took the midnight to four a.m. shift so Bill could get some sleep. As Topher lay next to his mother, he could hear her stop breathing for a while, gasp, and then resume breathing. This Cheyne-Stokes Respiration pattern is typical of someone in the dying process. At four o'clock, Topher's wife Katy relieved him.

After an early breakfast at my niece's, I drove back to Bill and Diane's house. Riding with me was their only granddaughter, four-year-old Tessa, and their two-year-old grandson, Teliz. On the drive, the kids belted out a Northwoods canoeing song they had just learned.

"Can we sing this for Grandma Di-Di?" Tessa asked.

"Yes, of course," I said. "Your grandma has always loved canoeing in the wilderness. She'd like to hear your song."

When we arrived and climbed the stairs to the bedroom, Diane was in fresh, pink-flowered Capri pajamas. Her eyes were closed. She seemed to be resting comfortably.

"Good morning, Katy," I said. "Good morning, Diane. It's Nancy. Tessa and Teliz are here, too."

Diane didn't respond.

"They've been practicing a song they'd like to sing for you. Would you like to hear it?"

Diane immediately pushed herself to a sitting position and swung her legs over the side of the bed. Blond-haired Tessa and Teliz stood side by side, looking up at their grandmother's face, and sang softly.

Land of the silver birch
Home of the beaver
Where still the mighty moose
Wanders at will.

Although Diane kept her eyes closed, she leaned toward the children and appeared to be listening intently. Their voices grew more confident:

Blue lake and rocky shore,
I will return once more.
Boom-diddy-ah-da, Boom-diddy-ah-da,
Boom-diddy-ah-da, bo-oo-oom.

After another verse, Tessa and Teliz giggled with pleasure at their performance and scampered downstairs, calling back "Bye, Grandma Di-Di!" Diane lay back down on her side.

Katy looked tired. She had been with Diane for almost four hours. I told her that I would take the next shift. We didn't realize it would be the last one.

I joined Diane on the bed, my face less than a foot away. I marveled at her clear, supple skin and generous lips.

Suddenly Diane opened her eyes and gazed directly at me. The deep blue of her irises against the bright yellow-gold of her eyes still astonished me. During the past nine weeks, I had not gotten used to what liver failure had done to her skin and eye color.

As Diane stared at me, I started to feel uncomfortable. Did she need anything? Did she want to say something? Did she even see me? Gradually her gaze soothed my fears and answered my questions. I could see no anguish in her eyes, no suffering or sorrow. I sensed a deep, calm spaciousness. It was like looking through her eyes into eternity. I settled down inside and let myself be still with her. For long, precious minutes, we just gazed and breathed together.

Then Diane pushed herself back into a sitting position and swung her legs over the side of the bed, her bare feet on the floor. I got off the bed and faced her. She reached up and pulled my head to her shoulder. I had seen Diane do this with Bill the night before when he had helped her stand. Thinking she needed to use the bathroom again, I started to straighten up. But Diane clamped down on my neck. She *was* strong!

"Do you want me to stay like this for a while?" I asked.

She didn't respond.

I was bent almost 90 degrees at the waist. After a minute, my back was aching.

"Diane, this position isn't comfortable for me. If you want some support to stay sitting up, I could get behind you, and you could lean back against me. How would that be?"

Immediately Diane's hands dropped to her lap. I crawled onto the bed behind her, spread my legs, and pulled her snug against me so that her legs stretched out between my legs. She leaned back against my chest, her cheek touching my cheek.

For the next two-and-a half-hours, that's how we stayed. It was one of the most intimate and sacred experiences of my life. It was an honor to hold her, support her, breathe with her, love her.

After a while, I heard words in my mind. I pushed them away. Diane didn't need any words. After all, she was engaged in one of the most profound labors of her life. But the phrases kept coming, and eventually I trusted them. If Diane wanted me to be quiet, she would let me know.

"That's right, Diane . . . Just let yourself relax . . . I'm right here with you . . . You don't have to do anything . . . You can relax and let go . . . ."

I sensed a little release of tension in her body. I was calm and steady, as if I had been with a dying person many times. In fact, it was the first time.

I felt grateful for the three years of Living in Process training I had done with psychologist Anne Wilson Schaef. This self-directed healing work included hours of sitting on a mat beside someone who was allowing repressed feelings to surface, supporting them in their deep emotional release process. I had learned to trust my intuition about when to be a silent witness and when to say something encouraging or reassuring. Sitting with Diane felt similar.

"You know exactly how to do this, Di . . . Just like you knew how to be born."

I wasn't trying to think of anything to say, but from time to time, words spilled into the companionable, luminous stillness.

"Everything's going to be fine, Diane . . . *You* are going to be fine . . . In fact, you're going to be *more* than fine . . . You're going to be free of any struggle, any pain, any itching!"

I could feel her relax more deeply. We were breathing together, eyes closed, comfortable.

"You'll know when the time is right to leave . . . You can do it in your own time and in your own way . . . Just relax and follow the process on out . . . ."

I figured it would be several more days. Surely anyone strong enough to wrap her arms around my neck in a vice-like grip wasn't close to dying.

At ten o'clock, after almost two hours, I said, "I just want to let you know that I have a half hour left to be with you. Becky is arriving at ten-thirty to drive us to Madelia for lunch with our moms. If there's anything you need before I leave, just let me know in whatever way you can."

Diane gave no response.

I resumed the rhythm of comfortable silences and the occasional words that seemed to come not so much *from* me as *through* me. I didn't even know if I believed all the words, but I felt compelled to say them.

"You're almost home, Diane . . . All those you have loved will be there to welcome you . . . your mother, your father, the baby you lost . . . They will be so happy to see you . . . Everyone is waiting for you . . . You'll be home free, Diane . . . *Home free.*"

At ten-fifteen, Bill came upstairs. He kissed Diane, looked at my position supporting her, and asked, "Are you comfortable?"

"Pretty comfortable," I replied. Actually, my back was starting to tire.

He propped pillows around me, which felt wonderful, and mentioned that Diane's closest friends were coming between ten-thirty and eleven o'clock. He pulled a chair up to the foot of the bed, leaned forward, and tenderly took his wife's left hand.

At ten-thirty, I glanced at the clock. Since there was no sign of Becky, I stayed in place, holding Diane. Our chests rose and fell together.

"That's it, Di, just trust the process. Mmm-hmm. Home free. *Home free.*" It was so effortless, I felt as if I could stay with her forever.

Katy, refreshed from a nap, came back upstairs. "How's it going?"

"We're doing well," Bill said.

"I'll be leaving as soon as Becky arrives," I told her.

Katy went downstairs to ask Bill and Diane's son or his wife to take my place.

Tim and Kate both came upstairs. Tim sat by the bed and, taking his mother's right hand, put his fingers on her wrist, as he would have done with one of his patients.

"Her pulse feels thready," he said.

Kate studied Diane's face, left the bedroom, and asked everyone to come upstairs. She started the music Diane had chosen to die to, *Bach for the Bath*. The first piece was full, slow, intense. After several measures, a plaintive cello entered.

"Oh, Diane," I said. "There's your beloved cello."

More family members had gathered around. Everyone was quiet, listening to the soaring music. Suddenly I felt Becky behind me on the bed, one hand on the center of my back, the other on Diane's arm.

As the Bach piece came to a slow, peaceful close, Tim touched his fingers to Diane's wrist again, then to her neck.

"I don't get a pulse," he said.

Everyone looked at Diane, unable to take in Tim's words.

"But she still seems to be breathing," he observed.

Diane's chest was rising and falling, slowly, steadily. After a minute, Tim touched her neck again. "I think that's Nancy breathing. She's gone."

It was true. She was gone.

Bill, still holding Diane's hand, put his head on their joined hands on the bed and sobbed, "Thank goodness, thank goodness." After days of yearning for death, Diane had finally been released.

Although we all were crying, I felt strangely calm, full, saturated with the sacred mystery of the moment.

"You did it, Diane," I murmured, tears running down my cheeks and wetting Diane's still warm cheek. "You did it. You're home free."

Nancy Manahan, PhD, is a community college English teacher, now retired. She and her wife Becky Bohan have published five books, including the best-selling memoir *Living Consciously, Dying Gracefully: A Journey with Cancer and Beyond*. They are founding members of the Minnesota Threshold Network, which does education and legislative reform for family-directed after-death care and green burials. Nancy and Becky make their home in Minneapolis.

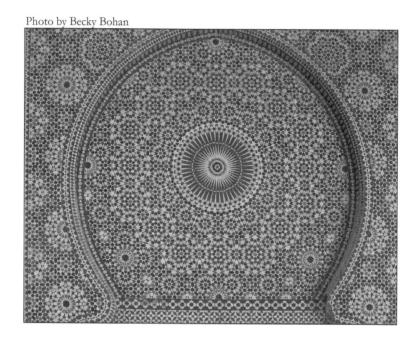

Portal-like tile ceiling in Fez, Morocco.

*"I was experiencing something I'd never seen before—a person's death
—and something I didn't know could happen—
the other world opening to receive a spirit."*

THE PORTAL

BECKY BOHAN

On Saturday morning, I was supposed to be 75 miles south of Minneapolis at 10:30 a.m. to pick up my spouse, Nancy. She had been visiting her brother Bill and his wife Diane, who had end-stage breast cancer. Nancy and I had planned to drive to our hometown, 25 miles farther, to take our mothers out to lunch at eleven o'clock.

But I procrastinated. I puttered, straightened up the desk, searched for the car keys, and organized my fanny pack. My usual need for punctuality was oddly absent.

By the time I left Minneapolis, I knew I'd be late. But Nancy's motto, "Trust the process," began to play in my head, and I relaxed. So what if I arrived a little late?

As it turned out, I reached Bill and Diane's house at 10:40. Ten minutes late. Big deal, I thought, as I pulled up to the house and saw their son David and his wife Jill sitting on the front steps. I waved and entered through the side porch, carrying the Indian meal Nancy and I had cooked for the family the day before.

But those extra 10 minutes *were* a big deal. They gave Diane a chance to die in Nancy's arms.

I had put the food in the refrigerator and was turning to leave the kitchen when someone called down the steps. I couldn't hear the words, but I saw the shock on David and Jill's faces as they came inside. I hurried after them up the stairs, joining the other children and spouses in the master bedroom at the top of the stairs.

I beheld a beautiful scene. Diane was sitting crosswise on the bed, leaning back against Nancy's chest. Bill held his wife's hand and their son Tim, a doctor, had his fingers on her other wrist. Nancy was murmuring, "That's right, Diane, relax and just let go," as a Bach cello prelude played in the background. I joined Nancy on the bed, one hand on her back and the other on Diane's arm. Tim

73

checked for a throat pulse. Everyone waited, trying to believe that what they were seeing was really happening.

"I don't get a pulse," he said finally." "But she still seems to be breathing."

It was true. Diane's chest was rising and falling.

After another minute, Tim said, "I think that's Nancy breathing."

He checked again for a pulse.

"She's gone."

Bill put his head on Diane's hand and sobbed. Nancy continued to hold Diane in her arms, whispering, "You did it. You're home free. You're home free."

By this time, everyone in the house was in the bedroom. We entered a kind of altered state where shock, disbelief, grief, and relief blended.

Tears flowed and ebbed and flowed again. Bill and Diane's four-year old granddaughter Tessa climbed on the bed and sat next to Diane. I wasn't sure if she understood what was going on, but as she broke into sobs, it was clear she knew that her beloved, 60-year-old grandmother was gone. Other family members crowded on the bed until it was a float of love and grief.

After several minutes, I eased myself away from Nancy's side and slid off the bed, letting others move into my spot. The grouping reminded me of a nativity scene, with friends and family gathered to mark a momentous transition. But instead of welcoming a newborn, we were witnessing an old soul depart.

I wondered what Diane was experiencing. Was her spirit still in the room?

I thought about people who have had near-death experiences. Most of them say they rose up and looked back down at their body and at the people tending to it. I wondered if Diane was looking down on us at that very moment. Was she elated that she was finally free? Sad to see us crying? Curious about what we would do with her body?

I looked up and greeted her silently: Hi Diane! You did it!

As I gazed at the white, textured ceiling directly above Diane's body, I became aware of something extraordinary. The ceiling looked solid, yet it wasn't. There was a passageway a little smaller than a manhole, some sort of portal.

I was transfixed and stared at it for a minute or two. After a while, I looked around the room, wondering if anybody else had seen the opening in the ceiling. But everyone was intent upon the death bed, silent or softly crying. I wanted to blurt out, "Does anyone see what's happening above the bed?" But the words wouldn't come. To speak aloud seemed not only disrespectful, but also an intrusion into each person's private experience of grief.

And what if no one else saw what I was seeing? I could hardly believe it myself. I was a businesswoman, the vice president of the company I had started 15 years earlier, a bottom-line type of person geared to facts and figures. A hole in the ceiling? People would think I was not only disrespectful, but crazy. I stayed silent, but continued to look upward.

On the other side of this portal, three beings were propped on their elbows around the opening, looking down on the scene. Only their heads appeared and, occasionally, their necks, as they seemed to lean in for a closer look at times. They all had definite, but ethereal form—they were male, completely bald, wrinkle-free, but ancient.

The three stayed in their positions, equidistant from each other, but they seemed to shift occasionally on their resting arms. They exuded utter peace and infinite patience. They gazed down as if looking into a well, waiting for a friend to climb up. They didn't extend a hand or cross the threshold of the open portal. They only waited. They made no sound. All of their attention was focused on Diane.

I wondered if one of these spirits was Diane's deceased father, Mr. Jansen, my eighth-grade geography teacher. But none of them resembled him, and besides, these beings seemed incredibly old.

I longed for Nancy to join me so I could show her what I was seeing. Once, when someone stood up from the bed, I claimed a spot next to Nancy. I asked her if she wanted to stay in that position, hoping she wanted relief. But she said she was fine, and I realized she couldn't yet leave Diane. I looked up to the ceiling from the bed. The portal was still there with the three beings. I could not sense anything beyond them.

Again I stood back from the bed. I continued to observe Diane's body in Nancy's arms and the portal directly above them. I was experiencing something I'd never seen before—a person's death—and something I didn't know could happen—the other world opening to receive a spirit.

As I continued to watch the portal, I recalled a book I had read a couple of years earlier written by two Mayan scholars.[1] The book described sacred

---

1   Linda Schele and David Freidel, A Forest of Kings: The Untold Story of the Ancient Maya. New York: Quill, William Morrow, 1990.

rituals that the Mayans believed dissolved the veil between this world and the next and enabled them to commune with their ancestors in the Otherworld. I suddenly realized that the portal above Diane must be what the Mayans were able to summon through ritual. It was their door to the spirit world.

The revelation staggered me. I was glimpsing a whole different plane of existence, a place of deep, cosmic wisdom. I felt in my bones that ancient people—the Mayans, Greeks, Egyptians—knew of this passageway and opened to it in their sacred ceremonies.

I'm not sure how long the portal stayed open. Time was not flowing at its normal pace. If I had to guess, I'd say about 20 minutes. During that time, people moved around the room, some left to make calls, others joined the gathering. Eventually the portal started to fade.

I left the room when Diane's body was to be washed. As I descended the steps, I hung onto the railing, my knees wobbly. Downstairs I sat alone in the living room, shaken to the core. I couldn't separate the emotional impact of Diane's death and the spiritual impact of the portal. They were the two sacred streams of my experience with Diane's transition, irrevocably entwined.

When I returned to the master bedroom an hour later, Diane was on the bed, wearing the blue dress she had chosen for this occasion, her hair combed, fresh lipstick applied. Candles were burning, and the room was ready for the family members and friends who had started to arrive.

The portal was gone.

Later that day as I mulled over the entire experience of Diane's death and the portal, a few thoughts came to me. First, that my high school English teacher was wrong. He would say on occasion, "We are born alone and we die alone." As a teenager I accepted such existential angst, but as an adult, I came to believe the first part was nonsense. Born alone! Excuse me, where is the mother in all of this? When we slip through the birth canal, it's a joint effort. A birthing baby is literally surrounded by her mother! And except in rare cases, there are ready hands waiting to catch the newborn, to lift her to a new place on earth, to tend to her immediate needs, and to place her in her mother's arms, where she can be comforted in this new world.

But now, after witnessing the death of Diane, I know we do not die alone either. Even if our passing is on a solo trip in the Amazon or up the snowy sides of Mount Everest, when the time comes, others will be gathered at the end of a different type of birth canal to enfold us and welcome us to a new home. *We are not alone.*

I realized also that death, like birth, is a process. Diane told Bill in her last days, "I'm ready to die, but I don't know how to." Just as her baby self knew how to slide down the birth canal, however, when the time came, Diane's adult self knew how to handle the departure of her spirit into the ethereal passageway. Ultimately she didn't need to do a thing, except find a way to let go. The process happened in its own time, in its own way.

Shortly after Diane's death, I read in *Graceful Exits: How Great Beings Die* that Buddhists like to die sitting up so that their spirit can more easily emerge from their seventh chakra, through the crown. This is exactly the position that Diane chose. She may not have known why, but her body and spirit guided her.

I have learned that my experience with the portal is not unique. Others have sensed the presence of a passageway at the time of death. I know now that such a doorway exists and that a gentle, loving reception is ready for all of us when our moment is at hand.

BECKY BOHAN, MA, is a retired small business owner. She and her wife Nancy Manahan have published five books, including the best-selling memoir *Living Consciously, Dying Gracefully: A Journey with Cancer and Beyond.* They are founding members of the Minnesota Threshold Network, which does education and legislative reform for family-directed after-death care and green burials. Becky and Nancy make their home in Minneapolis.

Jody Kristine Johnson is pictured here with her dearest friend,
Michelle Mitchell-Miller Michelle, who is now dancing with the angels
until they meet again.

"I always told Michelle she was my purple orchid—
unique, delicate, but incredibly strong."

ORCHID

Jody Kristine Johnson

I met Michelle when we were both pregnant with our first child, nearly 20 years ago. A fiery redhead, she was a fluid, passionate flame of a person— always glowing and in constant motion. Her searing intelligence and slightly twisted sense of humor drew me to her immediately, and we quickly became close friends.

I always told Michelle she was my purple orchid—unique, delicate, but incredibly strong. She was like one brilliant purple orchid in a field of dandelions—someone completely herself in a world with too much uniformity. Someone who was born to stand out. Michelle was a flaming redhead with a near genius IQ who turned heads wherever she went.

We raised our children together over the years, shared our hopes and dreams, supported each other in our various life challenges. We both had children with special needs, our oldest daughters both exhibiting attention deficit disorders, one son each born with an autism spectrum disorder. We were inseparable, and jokingly planned for the day when we would be "two eccentric old ladies sitting on the front porch together, in matching rocking chairs." On the last day of June in 2008, I talked to her on the phone, as I usually did each morning. She ended our daily conversation the way she always did, with "I love you—talk to you soon."

The next day she was dead, at the tender age of 39. Her 15-year-old daughter had found her in bed, not breathing. Later we were told that her heart had stopped, an unforeseen reaction between two prescribed medications for a chronic brain condition that she had twice had surgery for.

I had never pictured the rest of my adult life without her, and the intensity of my grief washed over me like a recurring tide for months. That tide awakened an energy in me, a raw, primal power that pounded through me, demanding expression. That first year, I found myself cleaning and painting each of the rooms of my house. I picked vibrant colors in an effort to recreate my external world, a world that had been inexorably changed by her absence. I began to work for hours each day in my yard, mowing and trimming bushes, planting a flowering crabapple tree with deep red blooms that reminded me of Michelle's flaming red hair.

Later I added a bench under that tree, and continued to add new flowering plants to what became a living memorial garden. There were pink and white peonies by my back stairs, Dutch tulips and crocuses by the sandbox our children had played in. I planted distinctive blue irises along the fence line, and lilies of the valley by the garage.

I found myself creating in other ways as well, finishing a book of poetry I had begun before Michelle's death, which included a dedication to her. I gave copies to her husband and parents. Her mother later described reading individual poems out loud to her husband (Michelle's father) as he sat in his easy chair on the long evenings after her death. She shared how much this tribute to their daughter had moved them in those quiet moments. I went on to write and self-publish two additional books of poetry, both of which included dedications to Michelle, as well as other family members and friends. In one poem, I described my burgeoning creativity after her death as "invoking daffodils in her name—thousands of yellow daffodils pulsing out of my hands like flames."

I expanded into writing essays, and had several accepted for anthologies that revolved around depression and anxiety—issues that had been lifelong challenges for both Michelle and me. I accepted an invitation to be part of a panel on mental health issues at a local university after years of avoiding public speaking. Somehow her death had invoked in me qualities she had seen in me that I had not fully seen in myself. When Michelle was alive, her gift to me was her love and attention, her encouragement and support. After her death, I believe one of her gifts to me was the growing confidence I had in myself and my abilities. Confidence she had had in me all along. Her constant affirmation of my strength, intelligence, creativity, and courage became tools of growth that I claimed more fully after her death. I found myself growing and stretching into new activities, taking on more ownership and leadership in my life.

Shortly before she died, Michelle had told me how glad she was that "I was coming into my own." At the time, she had meant gaining networking and social skills that had long eluded me as a younger woman. After she died, her words blossomed into something more encompassing. It was as if the inspiration of her strong and loving spirit had given me permission to utilize my own strength, to take steps into the previously unknown that I might never have attempted before. I felt for the first time that I was not only able to walk outside of my comfort zone, but to dance.

Michelle died before she was able to do some of the things we had planned as young women. We wanted to travel, to write our memoirs, watch our children grow up and become independent. I had done very little traveling when our children were young, other than a few short family trips. It was too difficult to travel easily with four young children, and my anxiety complicated the idea of any extensive travel. I preferred to stay close to home, where I could better control my environment.

After Michelle died, I bought a medallion engraved with a picture of the two of us, and in her memory I started to go a little further afield. I started small, driving to Duluth from Minneapolis with a friend. I visited the extensive rose garden there, wandering among the flowers and remembering how Michelle had loved roses, how I had sent a dozen to her each year on her birthday. At the rose garden, I took pictures of hundreds of varieties of roses. I went on to visit Seattle for a friend's wedding, taking the ferry from there to Victoria, Canada. It was the first time I had ever been outside of the United States. I toured a castle there, rode in a horse-drawn carriage, had my picture taken with a wooden moose in front of the local shops. Everywhere I went, I wore the medallion with our photo. As long as I wore that medallion, I felt that Michelle was with me, at least in a symbolic way. That through me, she was able to visit some of the places she had never been.

Last year I flew to Chicago for the first time, to attend a science fiction convention. I travelled alone, met some of my favorite television actors, and had my picture taken with them. I visited Navy Pier and rode the train for the first time. I got an autograph from an actor I had long admired, and told him how much his performances had meant to me while shaking his hand. Through it all I wore the medallion, and in some small way felt that Michelle shared those experiences with me, and was delighted that I had taken the risk of making our youthful plans a reality.

I still wear that medallion. Our first-born children are adults now, and I wore that medallion to their graduation parties. Her daughter recently became a massage therapist, and mine is in her first year of college at a local university. Our younger children are adolescents, growing older and stronger every day. Her family keeps in regular contact with me, and I attend many of their family gatherings. I tell her children stories about their mother and I when we were younger, stories about themselves in their early childhoods. I try to keep her memory alive for them, reminding them of the strong and vibrant woman that she was, of the deep love she had for them. I am part of their earliest memories, and they find a part of their mother in my eyes and in my heart. I watch them grow up now, knowing that even though Michelle is no longer physically with us, her love remains. I know that the force of that love forever changed those of us who were closest to her, and that its essence lives in the hearts of her children.

My memoirs still wait to be written. Michelle's are written in the people who loved her, and in the faces of her children. They are written in the lives of the many people she has touched with her insight, courage, and compassion. Michelle's memoirs will continue to be written as those of us who loved her live out our lives, remembering the strength of her enormous spirit, and honoring the depth she brought to our hearts.

JODY KRISTINE JOHNSON has a master's degree in community counseling from the University of Wisconsin-River Falls and works as a child protection social worker. She has previously self-published four books of poetry on the site lulu.com: *Anam Cara, Communion, Touchstones,* and *A Place in the Sun.* She has also been a contributor to two recent anthologies, *Not Alone: Stories of Living with Depression* (Civitas Press, 2011) and *Anxiety Disorders, True Stories of Survival* (Hidden Thoughts Press, 2012). She lives in Richfield, Minnesota, with her husband, three of her four exceptional children, and assorted furry pets.

Marilyn Strong

*"The experience of Sara's death and the facilitation of her
memorial service were the transitional events that
planted the seeds for a new expression of my work."*

DEATH: FROM FEAR TO EMPOWERMENT

MARILYN STRONG

I remember the first time I became aware of the reality of death. The year was 1962; I was in second grade, and not more than seven years old. I would walk 12 blocks to my grade school, outside the city limits north of Spokane, Washington, and was often accompanied by my older sister, Cheri. During this walk I would always see a young girl, about my age, from a distance, walking with a nurse or a nanny. What first caught my eye was her size; she was unusually overweight for a girl her age.

There was also something mysterious about her, for she lived in my neighborhood and yet I never saw her at school. She was never alone on these walks, in that she always had an adult with her, and yet she was always alone, in that I never saw her with other children. I often thought about her, and wondered if she was lonely, but I was too timid a child to introduce myself and befriend her. I eventually discovered that she suffered from leukemia, and that the medicines she took caused her to gain the weight. I never knew her name, and only saw her on her walks, on my way to and from school.

One day I realized that I had not seen her walking for several days in a row. I don't recall how I found out, but word came that she had died. The finality of it began slowly sinking in, and my innocent sense of well-being came crashing down around me. Death did not just come to old people! Someone my age could, and has, died! Suddenly, I realized that it could also happen to me. I remember going to my mother in her bedroom, lying on her bed, sobbing, trying to explain to her what was wrong, longing for consolation that I knew in my heart of hearts she could not give. This was a hurt she could not kiss away. The world shifted for me that day in an irrevocable way. I was crying, not only for the unnamed, unknown girl, but I was crying for the recognition that some day I, too, would be no more on this earth, and I was afraid.

That fear of death stayed with me throughout my childhood and into my middle adulthood, primarily because, like most of us in this culture, I was not taught experientially about the natural cycles of life and was protected from any direct contact with human death. The first funeral I attended was for my paternal grandmother when I was 14. I never got to see her dead body before she was buried. Death was such a scary thing precisely because it was so mysterious and unknown to me, and I was so inexperienced with it. We humans tend to be afraid of things that we don't know, and therefore don't understand. The truth is that our culture teaches that death is something to be ignored, denied, feared, and avoided as much as possible. We try to insulate ourselves from the reality that death is a natural part of the cycle of life.

As a young adult I moved to Whidbey Island, Washington and studied Native American and European earth-based spiritualities, and through the teachings of the medicine wheel came to know more intimately about the life-death-life cycle ever present in the seasons of the year. In my mid-30s I experienced a metaphorical death through the loss of a 10-year marriage that I valued. This shattering led me to explore many of the classic descent myths. The myths helped me, after much resistance, to befriend the surrender and letting go process that is inherent in any death, be it physical or metaphorical. Although it took me many years to heal from that experience, I did emerge with a stronger sense of self and a belief and deeper understanding of the promise of renewal that follows any death. I eventually came to see the divorce as one of the most valuable experiences of my life. I was becoming more familiar with the territory of death. However, it wasn't until I was in my early 40s that I had the privilege of being present at the physical death of a dear friend, Sara, in 1997.

Sara had been a participant in the first year of a women's spiritual growth group that I co-created and co-facilitated with my friend and business partner Renie Hope called Gaia Spirit Rising: Healing Ourselves, Healing the Earth. From the fall of 1989 to the spring of 1990, Sara, along with 15 other women that year, gave herself fully to nine months of gathering weekly together, sitting in circle, and exploring issues of spiritual, cultural, and personal transformation through study, discussion, movement, creative expression, drumming, chanting, and sacred ceremony. Sara, like most of us, had grown up a daughter of the patriarchy, in a male-defined religious institution and identified fully with masculine ways of being successful in the world. Like many women, Sara was searching for a "God who looked like me," and she used the Gaia curriculum and experience to find a new source of empowerment for the second half of her life. Sara especially loved the chanting and drumming that I would lead at the beginning of each gathering.

Renie and I had created the Gaia program from the ashes of our failed marriages and the ending of our close association with the Chinook Learning Center, located on the south end of Whidbey Island, Washington. We had been covenant members of the Chinook community for many years and had worked together on the educational staff, facilitating both residential and nonresidential, nine-month-long programs. Major changes at Chinook, including the disbanding of the community, closely followed the exodus of our husbands from our marriages (ironically, within two months of each other). Our lives as we knew them were suddenly and irretrievably over. We were being kicked out of the "nest" and needed a new way to support ourselves financially. We also wanted to continue our in-depth educational work, teaching others how to create community, even as we created it for ourselves. We were participant-leaders, and Gaia became a crucible not only for the healing and support of the women who came to us but for our own healing as well. We went on to facilitate the Gaia program for seven more years, but there was something about that first group that bonded especially deeply. After the official end of Gaia 1, they continued meeting without us through the years, with Sara emerging as one of their strongest leaders.

Then, in the fall of 1993, Sara was diagnosed with cancer. We were informed that her prognosis was not good and her doctors gave her three to six months to live. Sara's one wish, at that point, was to live to see the birth of her grandchild. Her daughter, Jennifer, was newly pregnant at the time of Sara's diagnosis. Her Gaia group and the extended Gaia community rallied around to support her and her husband, Allen. Our support included hospital visits during her many surgeries, emotional support, healing ceremonies—creating ways to uphold Sara and to hold our own sense of shock and disbelief that this was happening to one of us, so young.

Months went by slowly as Sara grappled with the multitude of issues and decisions facing her. I had no easy answer when she asked my advice on whether to do chemotherapy. Initially she did do chemo, but soon wearied of the negative impact it had on her body and spirit. She then courageously chose to leave that known path sanctioned by Western medicine and began to trail blaze one of her own. She began working with a medical doctor who offered alternative treatments for cancer. More months passed. Sara's granddaughter was born, and she was overjoyed to have made it that long. Never once did I see Sara get caught in self-pity. She lived on, beating her doctors' timeline by three-and-a-half years.

However, in the spring of 1997, I received a phone call from one of the Gaia women telling me that Sara was well into her dying process, and that if I wanted to come to Seattle and say goodbye to her, I should do it soon. I was also informed that Sara had requested that I facilitate her memorial service. When I arrived that evening at Sara's home, she was surrounded by the sights and sounds of life; her hospital bed was in her living room, a makeshift altar nearby, candle flickering, casting shadowed light on fresh spring flowers, pictures of her loved ones and her special, sacred objects. The exquisitely beautiful and lovingly hand-crafted quilt made by her women's group hung nearby, each square a testimony to Sara's bright and giving spirit, and how cherished she was by each woman. Her family was there in support of her process and to grant her last wish, to die at home. There was a surprising lack of machines or medical equipment, save one computerized unit that dispensed pain medication slowly to Sara through an IV drip. At this point, she was refusing fluids and intravenous feeding, but the pain medication, given at regular intervals, helped her to rest more comfortably.

At first, the everyday atmosphere seemed to contradict what was happening. Amidst a backdrop of Sara's family chatting away over a supper brought in by another Gaia participant, Sara's slow, labored, and uneven breath was taking her step, by invisible step, closer to her passing. There was incongruence here, and yet a lovely perfection, for death is a part of life, as much as it may be denied by our culture.

I was honored to be included in this sacred leave-taking. However, I was feeling awkward, as I had never been so close to human death before, and because there was no private space to express my personal grief. I leaned over to whisper my assurance to Sara that I would be honored to facilitate her memorial service. I wanted her to know, so she would have one less worry. Yet as I spoke the words, I realized in her semi-conscious state that she was beyond the concerns of this world. Still, she opened her eyes, silently communicating to me that she understood and knew that I was there.

I sat next to her, longing to help ease her transition. I had brought my drum. The thought of drumming and singing to Sara had crossed my mind, but it was edited out by the impracticality of doing so in an environment where it might not be understood. Within just a few minutes of having this thought, Sara's husband, Allen, came to me and asked, "Would you be willing to sing some of the Gaia chants that Sara loves so much?" I was stunned, yet grateful for the synchronicity of the moment. I turned my attention briefly to Allen, acknowledging to myself what a fine, gentle, and good husband he was and how supportive through this four-year process he has been to Sara. I watched him wipe her brow, lovingly caress her dry, chapped lips with a moist sponge, and check her IV.

Relieved to have an avenue of expression for the mixture of joy and pain, sorrow and love I felt for Sara all at once, I began to sing. Suddenly the words of the chant written by my friend Betsy Beckman rang through with clarity and new meaning:

Mother Earth, Birth and Death,
Come and hold me in your arms,
Mother Earth, Life and Breath,
Come and hold me in your arms.
Cradle me, Circle me, Hold me in your Mystery.
Challenge me, strengthen me, Hold me in your Heart.

Chanting, the repetition of simple words and melodies over and over again, is an ancient practice developed to create sacred space.

As I was chanting, I was struck with the realization that I had done this for Sara before, during the Gaia program. Part of our curriculum had been the study of and a ritual reenactment of the ancient Sumerian myth of Inanna's descent to the underworld. During this ritual, I had stood by, chanting and holding the space consciously and with great care while she and others in the group descended, or "died." I had led her down through the seven gates to the underworld where she had released layers of her identity, one at a time, to each ritual gatekeeper. As Inanna, she had then "hung on a peg" until her body turned to "green, rotting meat" as it is described in the myth. Ultimately, as Inanna, she was brought the waters of life and restored through a ceremonial "long dance" to a renewed phase of her life.

Although a ritual and a metaphorical death, it had many of the same aspects of Sara's physical death that I was present to now. The story of Inanna is a death and resurrection myth, similar to the Christian myth, yet it predates Christianity by 2,000 years. This ancient myth involves goddesses and is told from the feminine perspective. We chose it as a fundamental aspect of our Gaia curriculum because it is such a potent template for a pattern of psychological and spiritual growth. Our hope was that by relating to this very early myth, from an age when the Great Goddess was still vital, that participants would be able to reclaim some connection to the archetypal feminine instinct and spirit that our culture sadly lacks.

I sang the chant of Inanna, (author unknown):

I am your child, oh Ancient Mother,
I am your child, oh Mother of the World.
I am your child, oh Ancient Mother,
I am your child, oh Mother of the World.
Ohhhh Inanna, Ohhhh Inanna, Ohhhh Inanna.
It is you who teach us to die, be reborn, and rise again.
Die, be reborn, and rise again; die, be reborn and rise.

During Sara's ritual death, I had stood in support of her process just as Inanna's trusted companion Ninshubur stood watch for her journey. During Sara's ritual death, I had led her with chant, prayer, and drum to help build a sacred container strong enough to carry her through to the other side. I could only pray that this small offering of drumbeat and chant now would provide her some of the same for this, the literal death of her body. The difference was that this time 1 would not be there when and where she reemerged to be reborn. I could only pray that there would be unseen and loving hands to greet her on the other side, for I knew in my bones that she would be reborn, just the same. I sang one of my favorite chants, taught to me by Rabbi Schlomo Carlebach:

Return again, Return again, Return to the Land of your Soul.
Return again, Return again, Return to the Land of your Soul.
Return to what you are, Return to who you are,
Return to where you are, born and reborn again.
Return again, Return again, Return to the Land of your Soul.

The chanting took me more deeply into a place of communication and communion with Sara than merely speaking to her could have. Her breathing quieted and her pain and agitation seemed to ease for a while. After an hour or so, I stopped. It was time for me to go. Remarkably, the rest of Sara's family had retreated upstairs, and I was now in a darkened room surrounded only by the quiet of Sara's breathing.

I returned the next day around noon, as soon as my work schedule allowed. I arrived to find that Sara had died only 20 minutes prior, and Ruthe, another of the Gaia group and a registered nurse, was there alone. It was time to bathe Sara's body and to prepare for her lying-in-honor. We did this together in silence or shared chanting. Not only did I find my personal fear around death being released through this experience, but I also felt incredibly gifted by it. It was heart opening, healing, and transformational.

When someone dies, the portal between the worlds opens, just as it does during a birth, and it is very powerful. I was transformed by being present to this energy, by touching, bathing, and dressing this woman who had been my friend, but who was now in the process of leaving the shell that was her physical body. Rather than being afraid, I found it to be a privilege and an honor to be able to tend to someone who has passed. Her spirit permeated the room during those initial hours after her death and during the hours that she lay-in-honor in her bedroom, allowing friends and family to come and say their goodbyes. However, her spirit slowly diminished and when the family was ready, she was taken to cremation. Eventually I felt Sara's spirit dissolve into all of nature, into everything, including myself. I took part of her away with me, and I no longer feared death. This was Sara's gift to me.

A second gift would come from this experience, unbeknownst to me. At the time of Sarah's death, I was grappling with another death—the ending of the Gaia program itself. We had created Gaia at the crest of the wave of the emerging women's spirituality movement. Now, after "riding" it for eight years, this wave had expressed its fullness, splashed on the shore, and was receding back into deeper waters. Enrollment for the program was down, but I had also grown weary of the work, as fulfilling as it had been. I had been leading nine-month-long groups for 16 years (the previous eight through Chinook), and something else was calling me forward, although I had no name for it. At the time, all I could feel was the grief of letting go. The form that enabled me to lead and participate in sacred ceremony, which had led me to my true vocation, was crumbling, and I had no idea whether or not a new form would take its place.

In fact, the experience of Sara's death and the facilitation of her memorial service were the transitional events that planted the seeds for a new expression of my work. For the first time, leading her memorial service, I experienced myself in the role of "priestess" in a more mainstream form. Shortly thereafter, I became ordained as an interfaith minister and have developed a small business facilitating weddings, rites of passage, and memorial services. Additionally, during these past 15 years, I have had several dreams about caring for the dead, have experienced the deaths of several more friends and acquaintances and become certified as a death midwife and home funeral guide.

Marilyn Strong holds a BA in religion and adult education and an MA in spirituality and culture. She has been a skilled creator and facilitator of adult spirituality programs for twenty-six years. She is an interfaith minister and a respected ceremonialist and singer. For the past 15 years, Marilyn has worked closely with clients to create customized sacred ritual and ceremony such as weddings, memorial services, baby blessings, or rites-of-passage. As a certified death midwife, she also provides services to families as a home funeral guide. She is a member of the National Home Funeral Alliance and is currently president of the Langley Woodman Cemetery Board on south Whidbey Island, Washington, where they have recently opened a section for green burial. www.handsofalchemy.com

John Sime riding Ginger as Rosemary follows along.

*"Down to the barn, trying to get caught up caring for my horses. Having
animals to tend really forces you along in your grief process. They don't
exempt you from anything because of family-related emergencies.
They will have that food, or knock down the fence to get it!"*

ONCE AGAIN I AM JOHN
JOHN SIME

As I stared out the window of Intensive Care Unit 7 where my father lay dying, I noticed a driveway and loading dock below. In a flash of recognition, I realized it was the old loading zone that Dad and I once used to remove bodies from Lutheran Hospital in LaCrosse, Wisconsin. It was the entrance we used when I first started working with Dad here at the funeral home. He and I used it one sunny afternoon in June 1976 when I was preparing to leave for Mali in the Peace Corps. He didn't much want me to go to Africa, and he told me so that day. But he knew I had to get out of this little town, at least for a while—see some of the world, be of some use. He went away from Readstown for a while during World War II, but he came and had been here ever since. I came back, too, and we worked together here for years.

I was making funeral arrangements with a family when the hospital called and ended even the fragile hopes we had clung to for days. They were a most understanding family, not at all put off by my sudden exit to tell my mother the bad news. "We are in the same boat now, John," one of the daughters said to me, with a hug.

Somehow, it was good therapy for me to work on the arrangements for that family's mother, while at the same time the plans for my father's took shape.

Local funeral directors stepped right in: Larson's in Viroqua embalmed him, and Vosseteig's in Westby helped with the service. My cousin, Dean Jacobson, a funeral director in Michigan, offered his help. Dean also brought a little light into the gloom with his recollection about the time he and Dad gave me a haircut. They set me on the embalming table, took an electric clipper, and spun me around. It worked, but Mother didn't speak to either one of them for days.

Since I left for the Peace Corps in 1976, I have kept a journal, sometimes making daily entries and other times writing nothing for days, or even weeks.

During intense times, my journal can become an hourly log. It has been with me for 20 years, through some great times and some sad times, including the death of my father, Henry Sime, in June 1996.

Sunday, June 23:

I was making funeral arrangements with the Martin family when La Crosse Lutheran Hospital called and reported Dad's death. The funeral will be conducted by Pastor Aimee Wollman, who accompanied us to La Crosse during last Wednesday's crisis, when Dad went into a coma. Many people visited Mother tonight. My sister Jan and I will stay with her tonight. It will be good for all of us.

June 24:

The funeral process churns . . . getting details done is therapeutic. It is satisfying to track down one pallbearer and get him to say "yes" after calling four or five different numbers.

June 25:

Jan and I will again sleep at Mother's house. Mom says she wants to try it alone tomorrow night. One good feeling about the funeral experience after the medical experience is that although we are grieving, we are once again people. While visiting the ICU, the staff, understandably, seemed to avoid eye contact with us and kept any chit-chat to a minimum. Since Dad's death, here in my hometown of Readstown I am once again "John". I'm getting hugs and misty-eyed handshakes. It's good to be from here. It's good to be home.

June 26, 11:22 A.M.

At the Martin funeral now, I can hear "Precious Lord" being sung in the chapel. When the service is over, we will go off to the cemetery, and the Larson and Vosseteig crew will move in and set up the visitation for Dad. At 3:30 p.m., we will come back over and take our seats among the mourners. Some of the cookies and donuts people have been bringing to Mother's, in the small town tradition, are now below in the family lounge. Pastor Aimee and I had a nice talk yesterday afternoon.

June 27:

Last night was a panoply of memory and emotion. One of the first through the line was Al Ward, a funeral director from Evansville, Wisconsin, who was in Dad's class at the Wisconsin Institute of Mortuary Science in Milwaukee, almost 50 years ago. Many former customers. Association connections. A few relatives, but fewer than there used to be. Pastor Aimee was so kind and thoughtful. Just right for Mother, woman-to-woman. Jim did a good job of embalming. He got out most of the swelling from the heart treatment IVs. Dad is wearing his Navy Memorial tie, and we put his American Legion cap, his campaign ribbons, and the battered instruments he used on Iwo Jima in the casket (to be removed later and kept as mementos). Someone stuck a can of Skoal chewing tobacco in his hand. It wasn't me. I told them to leave it in.

Later, same day: 11:17 a.m.

Making more funeral cards on the printer while Jim Larson and Dave Vosseteig haul Dad and the flowers down to Peace Lutheran Church. They won't let me do much of anything, which is good. I'm not sure I could get anything done.

June 28:

Jan and I will begin working on the thank-you cards. All those flowers! I guess Jim and Dave took them to local nursing homes, which is great. I wouldn't have been up to it. The funeral was moving and appropriate. Pastor Michael (Aimee's husband) read the lessons, which means that they had to hire a babysitter.

Sandy Skarda and Margaret Larson were great on that old Norwegian tear-jerker: "Behold the Host Arrayed in White" and on the "Marine Corps Hymn". Aimee's sermon included several stories I plied her with as well as her insights into the crisis she witnessed on Wednesday.

June 29:

Down to the barn, trying to get caught up caring for my horses. Having animals to tend really forces you along in your grief process. They don't exempt you from anything because of family-related emergencies. They will have that food, or knock down the fence to get it!

Lessons I've learned from Dad's funeral:

Be more patient with families who are late for appointments. They are getting phone calls and personal visits. They are more than a bit numb. They are understandably reluctant to confront even the concept, let alone the profession, of death.

Never overestimate the memory retention of a grief-stricken family. Truly at some point in the past few days, you could have told me anything and I would have agreed to it and not remembered a thing.

Make sure everyone is getting enough to eat.

After watching other funeral directors in action I got an idea for an exchange program for funeral directors, like exchange students, nurses, ministers. What about Northern funeral directors working for a week in Southern funeral homes? Or vice versa, East/West, America/Europe?

I sit in the lawn chair next to the barn and watch the sun set as I read the *Diary of Anais Nin*, Vol. VI, 1955-66, page 40:

"The primitives were so wise when they enacted rituals of possession by the dead. It proves they knew it happened. And they also knew how to prepare rituals for dispossession. The same thing takes place in us, the so-called civilized man, but is not externalized (we have rituals to bury the dead and then we believe the relationship is terminated.) We are not made aware of the time and place when they reenter our being, and install themselves in our souls."

I'm not sure if Dad has installed himself in my soul, and I don't really care. I do know I am glad we went through each and every ritual this small town offers for the burial of the dead. Our culture is coming to see more and more that human experience, "primitive" or "civilized," is all essentially the same, and that sometimes we have to sit back and let the ritual unfold. Only then can we go on.

JOHN SIME is currently working on a memoir called "Life of an Undertaker—Learning to Say Goodbye." He is also working on a book of poems, *Toubabou and Au Nord*, about his experiences in the Peace Corps in Mali and events in that country currently. He has been published in *Epitaph-News, Kickapoo Free Press, Verse Wisconsin, Hummingbird Review*, and *Rivers and Roots*. He is a graduate of the University of Wisconsin–Madison and the Kentucky School of Mortuary Science, Louisville, and is the owner/operator of Sime Funeral Home in Readstown, Wisconsin.

"I, of course, started wondering about all of those rabbit drawings over the calendar years and wondered what my father was thinking or feeling in those moments of simple creativity."

THE SOUL LEVEL

MOKASIYA

Recently I received a medium size box of calendars. They were calendars that my Dad had drawn pictures on, in ink, or added the temperature for the day, snow and rainfall amounts, or a descriptive word or two about what he saw outside his window. There were ink drawings as well, drawings of eagles, woodpeckers, and other birds, and rabbits, especially drawings of rabbits—rabbits kissing, rabbits fishing, rabbits sledding in the winter, and rabbits, sunbathing on the beaches of Hawaii. I, of course, started wondering about all of those rabbit drawings over the calendar years and wondered what my father was thinking or feeling in those moments of simple creativity. But he was no longer here to ask, and if he was, I imagine he might just grin with that blue twinkle in his eyes as if we both already knew the answer without speaking.

I began to feel and think more about his dying and his living in this world, and it still saddens me or makes me laugh, depending on the moment, though seldom do I cry in grief now about his body passing on some years ago. I feel grateful that he is no longer suffering, yet I would have enjoyed having him around for a few more years.

I wonder about me being the keeper of these calendars that nobody in our family has any interest or attachment toward, at least that is what I tell myself. The calendars have many beautiful photos on them, mostly of nature scenes, some old buildings, and a few people. I consider tossing them all into the trash, or burning them in a fire, or passing them along to someone else, but then I choose to start cutting some of the photos out of the calendars myself. Possibly I will glue some of them together on a vision board, and I decide to keep all the ink drawing for further study and contemplation, especially the rabbits.

Soon I begin to get a couple of small stacks of photos of sunrises, sunsets, ocean scenes, waterfalls, trees, birds, animals, ferns, river stones, a host of beautiful places gifted through the photographers' eyes, and so I find myself cutting out a photo of a seal swimming in the ocean, and suddenly I have a new feeling spill over me and my whole body. My senses feel deeply, aware and alive.

I stop and begin looking at the photo. In the photo, the ocean is blue-green and the seal is diving downward. Its fur is tan colored and partially reflects the blue-green of the vast ocean. It feels like its eyes are looking right at me. One side of its deep brown eyes takes on the shape and color of a white crescent moon. The seal's face seems to smile as if to say, "Come and swim, come and play with me, look closer."

The lower half of the photo is a deep black. It is the shadow edge of land, an underwater cliff. In the darkness of this photo I suddenly see the shape of fingerprints, and a fired pulse of light, of energy, charges upward through my whole body as I realize these fingerprints were once the skin of my father's body. I begin to remember his fingers and his hands in prayer, in planting flowers in his gardens, in carving basswood figures, that upon his passing I received his carving tools, his sketches, the essence of his carving energy mixing with mine, even though I carve stone instead of wood.

For several moments, I feel a shared deepness of my father's divine essence all around and all inside of me. I reach out onto the dark of the photo and press the seal of his fingerprints into mine, and, suddenly, we are joined together once again. The fingers, hands, hearts, and spirit speak in silence with the cliff edge, the great ocean, the seal, Father and I. This moment lingers within me throughout the day, and then I realize it was what I had asked for, that all communication be born out of the soul level. I did not realize it would appear like this. I feel so grateful and blessed by this gift.

And the rabbits, well, that is still to ponder with a twinkle in the eyes, a smile, and an open, gentle heart.

Mokasiya's writing and poetry is inspired from relationship in community and the inner workings of the soul, from the natural landscapes of living in the Driftless region of Wisconsin and his wanderings in the desert southwest. Writing gifted him a way to be in the world. He self-published three books of poetry: *When God First Laughed*, *The Shamans Dream*, and *Climbing a Mesa*. His poetry has been published in *Sacred Fire, The Edge, Rivers and Roots, Free Verse, Natural Communities* and *Poetry out of Wisconsin*. Blog: mokalightpoetry. wordpress.com; email: rivertink@yahoo.com

"If you looked at the photo of all of us that sunny June day, our beaming faces full of laughter and love, you would assume we had attended a family reunion instead of a wake."

GONE FISHING

Nancy Grace Rosen

My brother's smooth, white knuckles grip the wheel. His hands have run a printing press for 20 years. Dan's hands taught his only daughter to hit a baseball, and these hands in one moment blew our family apart. His sky-blue eyes stay steady on the road ahead.

Dan is 47, slender with a strong, athletic frame, six feet tall with strawberry blonde hair thinning from his temples to his crown. Sunburned cheeks camouflage the hives that have broken out along his cheekbones. I sit beside my brother; our sister Terry and his daughter Kylie are in the back seat.

Midday Arizona sunshine sparkles through the shimmering waves of water. Light dances along the surface of the lake, the deeper pools an azure blue with indigo centers.

"Look at the trees in the water," Dan points with his chin.

Lake Roosevelt has not been this full of water for many years. The embankment between the road and lake is flooded. My younger brother by 13 years is a Cancer. Children, home, and water are most important to him.

"And there's the dam," he says as we cross the bridge toward the boat ramp and camping grounds where our father's memorial service will take place. Our father died on leap year day, the last day of six weeks of chemo and radiation treatments after having a brain tumor removed the day after this past Christmas.

I look down at the map Esther, Dad's second wife for nearly 35 years, printed for us. We slow down to find the Coyote Pass turn-off. "This is it." I say pointing to the left. After Mother's funeral 30 years ago, I swore I'd never attend another one. Today peace prevails where rage once reigned, the horror of it all washed clean from torrents of tears once the dam in me broke several years after I suddenly lost my mother.

Terry lights a cigarette and cracks the window. Kylie sighs and rolls her window down. She is 11 and takes a picture with her cell phone of the first crank car window she's ever seen in the Avis rental. We park next to a huge canopy of a palo verde tree shading two picnic tables in the foreground with a beautiful view of the lake as the background.

Our blended family is organizing and setting out the food and items prepared for Jim Bocock's memorial service. Esther walks up and says she wanted a space closer to where the pontoon boat would be for us to board with Dad's ashes, but that area is completely full.

"I think this spot is perfect." I blurt out and immediately ask if Esther wants to move.

"It's too late now, this will have to do." She places my father's photo wearing his red velvet Shriners fez hat. Carefully she places two clear glass vases on either side. Diana, a daughter-in-law, brings over a big bucket full of three dozen deep red roses. The three of us remove the plastic wrap and rubber bands. I prick my finger on a thorn and swish it in the leftover water.

"It stinks that he's gone," my stepmother wails, "It is awful, just awful."

Her shoulders slump with the slapping of her arms against the sides of her legs as she begins to sob. Diana rushes to hold her. Everyone falls silent. A breeze rustles through fronds and leaves, water laps against the rocks at the nearby shore, and an RV generator rumbles in the camping space next to ours.

Terry whispers in my ear, "You read what we wrote. I don't want to feel ridiculous bawling my eyes out the whole time." I tell her it is good to let the tears flow. She shakes her head no.

Her comment reminded me of how African women join hands in their village to keen the loss of their loved ones. This culture embraces grieving and wailing as part of letting go, standing in a social circle, embracing and releasing their tears together.

I whisper to Terry, "We should have a crying huddle for those of us who cry easily. We cry it all out huddled together; no one has to spend so much energy trying to hold back the tears." In my mind, this would include Christy, a granddaughter, me, and Diana and Marcia, both daughters-in-law.

Terry shrugs her shoulders and scratches her arms. My younger sister is several inches shorter than I am. Her platinum blonde hair has thinned around her forehead and crown after surviving the alopecia she suffered as a teenager when I left home for college. She and I had seen each other during Thanksgiving holiday the year before. It had been 20 years since we had been together.

The four days my sister and I spent in Sedona prior to meeting Dan on Friday evening were important to both of us. Terry's husband had been having as many health challenges as our dad for about the same length of time. She had been working full time and trying to tend to her husband's medical needs during Dad's hospitalization over Christmas with the brain tumor. She called Dad once a couple of years ago when he was going into the hospital for quadruple bypass surgery.

Terry called to tell me she told him she loved him in case that was the last time they would talk with each other. I love you, three golden words never uttered in our house while we were growing up. It had been nine years prior since they had seen each other at Grandpa's funeral, when Dad and Esther sold the furniture Granny had promised to Terry.

This trip is the first my sister has taken apart from her husband since they were married the same month Mother died. She and Ronnie spoke over the phone several times each day. This respite from his care gave us the time together to unwind. We ate, walked, talked, shopped, and explored a few Red Rock Campground trails, swam in crystal-clear streams, and enjoyed the beauty and peacefulness of Oak Creek Village.

The last night of our stay, I ask my sister if I could have some drags off her cigarette. Before she offers it to me, she makes me promise I will not start smoking. I had been judgmental of both my brother and sister's habit of chain smoking after growing up with two smoking parents in the house. In between puffs of her menthols, she says, "You know, Nancy, I think it is time I forgive Danny for killing Mom." I drop my shoulders and sigh.

"I can't believe it has taken me this long to realize that I want my brother in my life." My heart soars, but I stay quiet and hold her hand.

"I barely spoke to him at Grandpa's funeral. He was a pall bearer, but I could barely look him in the eye let alone say anything, and that was nearly 10 years ago." She glances at me through her bifocals.

"I am finally ready to move on." I smile in the moonlight and squeeze her hand as we sit on my friend's front porch with Bell Rock's shadow looming behind the moon. Crickets chirp and locusts whir in the trees. I sit next to Terry in the dark, watching stars flood the sky.

We became sisters again during our red rock days, like little girls at times, regressing to shared memories of the rainbow pancakes Dad used to help us make on Sunday mornings when Mother slept in. He let us pick out what colors we wanted. Terry remembered it was mainly green ones she chose and continues the tradition with her granddaughter, Noelle.

Two days ago Dan and Terry talked for the first time after 27 years of silence. Friday night's drive to where our brother and his daughter stayed took a long time, what with traffic and getting turned around a few times. His eyes appear startled and he shakes a bit as he opens the hotel door to let us both in. Terry and Dan head for the back porch when Terry said she needed to smoke. I go to the bathroom. When I return, Dan is asking Kylie if she sees any resemblance between Terry and him.

She shakes her head slightly and says nothing. Terry does not appear daunted.

She offers, "Nancy's friends asked me when the last time was we were all together."

I couldn't recall when it was.

Dan looked at me and says, "I think it was when I was five and you left home for college." I stood stunned with remorse and said I came home after that. I was surprised he didn't recall the times I visited him in the reformatory and halfway house; perhaps he did, but he couldn't say, since Kylie doesn't know yet about the six years he had served.

When Terry and I were together, she told me she thought it was when we were at his trial. We didn't mention it in front of our niece.

"Let's go swimming," Dan suggested, and we all got ready to go to several of the pools. I had some emails to do, so I told them I would be over soon.

I walked down to the pools and found Terry and Dan soaking in water from their necks down in the farthest back pool. They got out, and my niece and I went to the slide and slid down one after the other. It was fun, but I didn't go again. I don't recall the details of what each of us had to say. I mainly remember that the volume of talking seemed loud to me. Probably Dan was nervous and Terry, too. I know I was. A few more cigarettes were smoked on the back porch, and we drove to go eat. Dan offered to drive, and we looked for a Mexican restaurant. It was a cantina, and we sat in a large booth, Terry and I on one side, Kylie and Dan on the other.

Dan suggests we get a pitcher of margaritas, and we fill up on chips and salsa. I feel content. It feels good and happy for the three of us to be together again.

Terry and I stand and help lay out the tablecloths and bowls Esther has prepared. When we complete setting everything out, Terry sits down at one of the empty tables and lights another cigarette, like it is her best friend. I go for a walk around the campground, asking for a sign from Dad. A sweet fragrance wafts through my nose, and I see little white flowers growing below a verde tree with long, furry fronds of golden yellow and white.

I pick a branch of each and place them under Dad's photo.

When I sit down, Terry says, "There's a cardinal in the tree right there." Kylie gets her camera. My niece is as tall as Terry, with shoulder-length blonde hair like my sister's used to be. Kylie hasn't uttered a word since Terry's comment in the car: "My niece probably doesn't like sitting next to her psycho aunt."

"There's the boat!" Esther's eldest son calls out. Terry tells Christy to drive over and pick up Esther so she doesn't have to walk the distance. She turned 80 in January, two weeks after Dad turned 77. Their shared Capricorn traits of being down to earth and practical no matter what enhanced their togetherness. Between Dad and Esther, all eight children, five of 13 grandchildren, and eight great grandchildren are at this memorial. Ben and Jeremy's six little boys from one to seven run toward us, buried in bright orange lifejackets. They rode over from the Marina on the pontoon boat rented for the day.

Ben, Esther's grandson and minister, calls us to form a circle around the tree. Dan stands and reads a poem, "Gone Fishing": "I'm going fishing with someone very special to a special fishing hole." His voice cracks into sobs at the lines "On this trip I will be reminded of the love I've shared with you. I'll throw out the line, and when it's time, each of you will take hold. It will be then that

I bring you up, so we can go fishing together again. When anyone asks you, where's Jim, tell them I've gone fishing with God."

It is my turn to share some gifts our dad gave us when Terry and I were small. "Dad had a sense of humor and the ability to make lemonade out of all the lemons in life. He taught us to ride a bicycle and water ski, and we were the only kids on the block with wooden stilts." I cried and read at the same time, looking at Esther so she could read my lips, since I talked more softly than she could hear.

Ben reads from the Bible and says his grandpa Jim would tell us if he could that loss is gain, death is gain. Terry and I glance at each other, not convinced Dad would say such a thing. Rex then shares that Dad was a good husband to his mom, and Marty said he learned a lot from Jim, and he had been a wonderful grandfather to his daughter Christy. Uncle Bill plays the harmonica and Christy sings "Amazing Grace" in a clear, resonant voice. We all sing the last verse together and pray with Ben.

The three of us and Esther's five children select a red rose. Esther picks up the box of Dad's ashes as we walk to the boat together. Doug, Esther's second oldest son, steers the boat to the middle of the lake and stops the motor. Esther begins to stand with the bag of ashes out of the box and begins to drop, thrusting the bag to me. She says, "You do it." I hold the bag by the top. Terry is next to her and assures her we don't need to rush.

The three of us stand up. "We will do it together," I say calling to Dan to join us as I open the back gate of the boat. We stand in a huddle around Esther as Dad's ashes spill out of the bag in a showering sheet of fine, whitish-grey powder. The ashes meet the lake, an underwater cloud forms, and all 12 of us throw our roses in the direction of the cloud.

I whisper softly, "May you fish forever, Dad." A deep peace fills the space in my heart where there had been an empty hole, sometimes aching over the three months since he died.

Esther speaks to all of us after we sat back down on the boat seats, "Jim would say, done is done."

"Look, the roses are following his ashes," Dan announces.

The crimson blooms float upon the surface, the cloud of ashes still distinguishable from the rest of the water. Dad asked to be fish food; we gave him what he requested. Esther sighs, the gate closes, and the motor starts up. The wind blows our faces and hair.

I see now it took Dad dying to bring the three of us together again and for me to realize I do have a family. I step out of the boat, feeling lighter, taller, and at the same time more grounded, embodying my father's steady, confident playfulness and my mother's creativity, courage.

If you looked at the photo of all of us that sunny June day, our beaming faces full of laughter and love, you would assume we had attended a family reunion instead of a wake.

For my brother, sister and me, our mother's death blew us apart and our father's ashes ignited a kinship of love for one another and brought us together again.

NANCY GRACE ROSEN, MC, MEd, served as a child and family therapist, school counselor, and developmental educator for 35 years. As a certified breath, chi, and tong ren therapist, she was the first residential rebirther on Hopi. Ms Rosen has facilitated groups in areas of her expertise: breath, creativity, shamanic and tantric energy work with a wide variety of adults across the country. Nancy has authored a series of e-Books, *Your Breath is a Portal: Bringing the Unconscious to Light* and *Forgiveness Beyond Time—The Other Side of Family Murder,* available at www.PureEnergyIntegration.com

Diablo Valley Threshold Choir singing at Hospice of the East Bay Memorial Service,
Ellen Doerfer is second from the left.

"Because of my involvement with the Threshold Choir,
I feel that I am making a difference, both to the community,
and in my own growth and fulfillment."

THE BIRTH OF
A THRESHOLD CHOIR

ELLEN DOERFER

I am a senior living in an active retirement community, with a comfortable lifestyle, and actively involved in volunteer activities and social groups, with much contentment in my life. I am actively involved in my church, the Unitarian Universalist Church in Walnut Creek, California. I teach in the Religious Education Program, am a pastoral visitor, and have been involved in small group ministry for several years. I also belong to a regional women's social group that meets four times a year; we consider ourselves "Sisters for Life". In my retirement community, I belong to a Wisdom Circle of seven women that meets twice monthly for friendship and companionship. I am active in our local Emergency Response Team as an entry coordinator and meet regularly with my entry of 32 individuals. So you can see that I have a lot of interaction with my community.

I come from a large family, and have several nieces and nephews, and in the summer of 2010, I made my trek to Michigan for the annual reunion. During that time, I visited my niece, Anne, and her family. Anne has always had a special place in my heart. She has always spread goodness and joy to all who knew her and was a person who exuded joy and happiness. She was going through radiation for a cancer that had spread to many body organs. I was amazed that she was still operating with her usual schedule, i.e., working with her selected high school students in the morning, going into Grand Rapids in the afternoon for radiation therapy, and then meeting with family to go into Grand Rapids for her son's baseball game in the evening. (This was a usual day for her!)

In March 2011, I was attending a retreat for Unitarian Universalist (UU) women in Napa, California. That weekend I was grieving the impending death of my beloved niece, Anne; unfortunately, I was not able to be there to attend to her and her grieving family. I was so filled with grief, and was not very present for most of the activities of the retreat. At the suggestion of a friend, who knew of my family situation and my grief, I signed up for a workshop called Threshold Choir. The members of the Napa Valley Threshold Choir put it on, and I found that we would be singing to each other, and experiencing the act of singing at the bedside of someone who was in need of healing or was dying.

The friend gently encouraged me to volunteer to be in the "chair," a portable chair with a comforting blanket. She informed the group of my grief and sorrow. My tears were so close to bursting out, and as I entered the chair, tears were streaming down my face, and I could not hold back the sobbing that had been held back since the time I heard of my niece's imminent death.

As they sang the songs "So Many Angels" and "I Am Sending You Light," I felt the incredible sensation of my sadness floating away, and a calm of acceptance flowing through my body. The voices of the group of six women who sang to me were so soothing, melodious, and vibratory that it instilled in me a state of bliss. One of the participants told me that she saw my countenance change from sorrow to peace as I was sung to. The relief was so immense, and so freeing, that I was moved to action, and told myself and those around me that I would bring this program to my own community. In talking to the members of the Napa Threshold choir, I found out how to make contact with the founder, and more details regarding the choir. The Threshold Choir website was also a helpful resource for knowing their purpose, choir locations, contact people, and songs.

When I returned home about 6 p.m. on Sunday evening, I called my family, who were all sitting at Anne's bedside. They informed me that she was semi-comatose and was near the end. I told them that there may be a Threshold Choir in Southern Michigan, and I would contact them to see if they could sing for Anne. I talked with Kate Munger, from Inverness, California, founder of Threshold Choir, and made a request for singing to my niece. Kate was unable to reach any choir members in Southern Michigan, but said she would sing to my niece over the phone! She made the call, and with the family all at the bedside, she sang over my nephew, Rick's cell phone. He was able to convey to the rest of the family of Kate's healing and soothing voice. It was a touching experience for all of them, and Anne responded nonverbally to the singing. This was at about

8 p.m. Michigan time. My niece died about four hours later. In my subsequent visits to family in Michigan, I have laughed and cried with them. I told them how I had been inspired to start a choir after this most incredible experience surrounding Anne's death, and they have been happy to hear of my ambitious project of starting a new Threshold Choir that all started with Anne.

What a legacy she has left! An overflow crowd at her church in Hudsonville, Michigan, where the family has resided for many years attended Anne's funeral. Anne was a special ed teacher at the local high school, and was revered by students and teachers alike. Most of the teachers and students attended her funeral, and many spoke of her specialness and the loss they all felt. The community has attended to her grieving husband and children, Erica, a senior in high school and Nick, an eighth grader, with support in many ways—dinners prepared, phone calls of love and concern, and heartwarming messages.

With this inspiration, the seed was planted. Soon I began the process of recruitment, and with the help of Kate Munger, we were able to set a date for a four-session Threshold Choir Introductory Workshop in Walnut Creek in March of 2012. Thirty-two women completed the workshop, and we currently have thirty members; five members have "graduated" and can officially sing at the bedside. I have received the gift of having all of these women as my Threshold Choir Sisters. There is a special bond that happens when you sing together with such a purpose of relieving pain and suffering. We sing to each other in the "chair" at rehearsals, especially when someone has a need to be healed. Members have voluntarily agreed to assume responsibility for the leadership positions needed to run our organization.

Throughout this process, I felt so empowered to make a difference in providing this service to the community. I volunteered to join the Rossmoor Inter-Faith Council, which is closely connected with the Contra Cost County Inter-Faith Council, and through this connection, we can publicize our choir to the community. We also have the hospice organizations and Medical institutions to draw on for contacts/requests in the community. Already we have sung at the Annual Memorial Service for Hospice of the East Bay, and have a date to sing for the Kaiser Hospice Memorial Service in October 2012.

My heart runneth over with all that has transpired in these past months, and the sense of accomplishment with the help of all the choir members and the community's response. I feel l have awakened to a new woman! The death of

Anne changed my direction in life, enriched my life, and gave me new purpose. When I visited the family in Michigan this summer I was able to share with Anne's husband Rick what has transpired in my life, and how Anne's death gave birth to the newest choir, the Diablo Valley Threshold Choir. We cried together and were beyond words, just shared tears. It was very healing for me to see how he and the children are managing without Anne's physical presence, yet she is there in all our hearts.

As a retired registered nurse, I can still give to the community in a way that is a healthy outlet for my giving nature. Because of my involvement with the Threshold Choir, I feel that I am making a difference, both to the community, and in my own growth and fulfillment. It is easy to just sit back and let others do it, but that is not the kind of person I want to be. I am in the process of learning the role of being bedside coordinator for our choir, where I will do the intakes on requests for our singing, and then match the clients and bedside singers. We are fortunate to have the assistance of a nearby Threshold Choir to help us get started in organizing the role, and I will gradually assume this responsibility. What a joy to be able to be out in the community in a fulfilling role to help improve the quality of life for those who will use our services. The choir's singing makes kindness audible, and we share a culture of compassion and respect for individuals at the threshold.

Ellen Doerfer is a retired registered nurse, living in Rossmoor, an active retirement community in Walnut Creek, California, of nearly 10,000. She taught nursing for several years, both in adult school and community college. The last 20 years of her career was in a hospital setting with outreach to the community in wellness promotion. In retirement, she has been teaching healthy lifestyle and meditation techniques for improved quality of life.

Fred kisses Laura Elizabeth while she sleeps,
shortly before he leaves to serve in the Gulf War

*"Laura, when she was pain free, had a gaze that seemed to be saying
she needed you, trusted you, and was relying on your gentleness."*

LAURA'S GIFT

ROSEMARIE GORTLER

Someone once said that a good stretch is worth an hour's sleep.
I don't know about that, but a good stretch felt good on that November morning. My husband and I were visiting our son, daughter-in-law, and grandchildren in Colorado Springs. It was early, before 6 a.m. The house was quiet. I sat on the couch, alternately stretching and sipping my steaming cup of coffee.

I love being alone for just a little while in the early hours. That's probably a result of having five children and very little time for uninterrupted thoughts. I had just enough of that quiet time when I heard my son quietly talking to our new grandson as he brought the baby down to me. I was delighted. The baby's mom had fed him. He was full, happy, and playful.

Frederick William IV—his name is longer than he is.

The baby grinned up at me and responded to my peek-a-boo play with real belly laughs. We did the "so big" game, and he thought clapping hands was a great way to spend time. We were having a wonderful time. Five months is such a cute age, but then, every age is cute to grandparents.

We played for a good while in the quiet of the morning. After a time, he began rubbing his eyes. I responded to his tired message by positioning him with his head on my shoulder. Humming softly into his ear, I began a rocking motion. In short time, he was asleep.

I leaned back, allowing myself the continuing pleasure of those precious moments as I enjoyed the warmth of his rhythmic breathing on my neck.

My thoughts drifted to the day before and some small talk with little Freddy's mother, my daughter-in-law Ellen. We were talking about Freddy and how active he was. We laughed about how little boys differ from little girls. Ellen noticed that boys bang things to make noise "just for the sound of noise." She remembered our granddaughters being more sedate in their play. I smiled, remembering that as babies, my three daughters were able to pass down their playpens in great shape, but our two sons demolished their playpens.

Ellen's expression had changed. She looked intense as she changed the subject to mention her hope that her Laura would not be forgotten. Her comment startled me, because we frequently talk about Laura Elizabeth. Laura "Liz," as I liked to call my granddaughter, was two and a half when she died. Memories flooded my mind . . . .

Laura had been a tiny, delicate little girl. Her deep blue eyes were like her daddy's. She had soft sandy hair, which her sisters liked to comb and arrange. Laura was a "special" child. She was born with a chromosomal abnormality that caused her to suffer seizures—sometimes one after the other—until your heart broke as you watched. But she had improved so much and the suffering had subsided following her last hospitalization.

When Laura was born, I was devastated at the thought that she would never get to ride a bike or to run and play. The pain was not only for Laura but also for our son, for Ellen, and for the suffering they would experience because Laura would suffer. I was also caught up in Laura not meeting society's standards and how the world would treat her. That devastation slowly changed to a determination to help her to accomplish everything and anything she could be taught to accomplish and to help provide for her future.

Laura, when she was pain free, had a gaze that seemed to be saying she needed you, trusted you, and was relying on your gentleness. When you held her in your arms, you responded to that gaze. I thought this was my own private thought until I watched my brother hold her the Christmas Eve before she died. He plays with children but just doesn't hold babies! Yet he held her for a long time that evening, looking at her with contentment and peace.

My most vivid memory will forever be that of watching my husband at Laura's hospital crib side, stroking her head as he told her that he would always be there to care for her. Laura drew out his love so completely, which in turn magnified my feelings towards him. Laura . . .

I held little Freddy tightly as my mind replayed the events of March 16, 1991, the day Laura died.

It was 6:45 a.m. when the phone rang.

"Fred called at 5:00 this morning. He's on his way home and he wants the mother of all parties. I told him that everyone would be at the airport to greet him at 5:00 this afternoon."

My daughter-in-law, Ellen, spoke excitedly as she described the yellow ribbons that she and a friend had tied to every tree that lined the street from the main highway along the several blocks to their home. She went over the menu for the party that was planned for Fred's return from the Gulf War. I assured her that I would bring a few salads and that we would leave our home at noon to make the two-hour trip to their home and then to the airport.

I could not stop grinning. I was giddy as I prepared coleslaw. I imagined Fred deplaning. For so many months, my husband and I sat up until all hours of the night watching the war on TV. Our hearts were heavy when casualties were mentioned. We were as frightened as everyone else who had a loved one over there.

But Fred was coming home now. I looked at my watch—It was 7:00 a.m. Thoughts about Fred, Ellen and the three children reuniting were flooding my mind. Their children, our grandchildren, were eight, six, and two years old at that time. Julie is the oldest, with Carolyn in the middle, and Laura as the family inspiration.

Laura had been hospitalized many times in her two years. During those times, Ellen never left her side except when Fred came to relieve her. Together they never forgot Julie and Carolyn's needs. Julie and Carolyn knew their way around Walter Reed Army Hospital almost as well as they knew their own home. They would show us where the candy machine was, lead us to the elevators, and take us to the cafeteria.

Laura was a little fighter. She made it through those crisis times and had been doing so well for quite a while. I smiled as I imagined Fred once again jogging through the park, pushing little Laura Liz in the three wheel-jogging stroller while Julie and Carolyn rode their bikes along side.

When your child is so sick, one smile will make your day. Fred and Ellen worked so hard for that smile. When Laura smiled, they glowed. I later discovered how common this is among parents of special children. Laura's disabilities were accepted and Laura was loved. She was a gift sent to inspire our entire family.

Now Laura was doing well and Fred was on his way home. He could jog in the park with his girls again. I chuckled as I went over Ellen's call and her excitement. What a day! Thank you Lord!!

The phone rang. The clock said almost 8:00 a.m. It was Judi, our daughter living in Illinois. Judi and her family would be the only missing family members at this party. I was expecting her call. Judi would probably be lamenting her absence.

I was not prepared for her dismissal of my greeting. "Mom, something is wrong at Ellen's house—what is it?" I attempted to assure her that I had spoken with Ellen earlier and that all was well. "Mom—listen to me. Something is wrong. There's a babysitter there and she tells me that Ellen isn't available. She wouldn't let me talk to the girls. Something happened. You and dad better get up there—now."

I quickly hung up and called Ellen. The babysitter answered and wouldn't allow me to talk to my grandchildren. I pleaded, "Please—I'm the grandmother and I might be needed. Did something happen to Laura?" She was quiet. "Should I come now?" She gave the phone to her husband, and he simply told me that we should come early.

We left immediately. Somehow my husband and I knew that the situation was ominous. The trip was an interminable blur. Our hearts ached for Laura and for our son, for our daughter- in-law, and for our granddaughters.

Our fears were real. When we arrived, Ellen was back home from the hospital emergency room. She was in shock. Her baby was dead. The death of a child is unnatural. Parents and certainly grandparents are supposed to precede children out of this world.

Ellen honored our request to go to the hospital to be with Laura for a few minutes. She called to tell the hospital staff that we would be coming to say "good-bye" to our little Laura Liz. We were told to meet the nurse in the chapel.

Within minutes, we were seated in the chapel awaiting the nurse. The nurse arrived carrying Laura, wrapped in a receiving blanket. That "angel of mercy" was as compassionate as could be as she offered us an opportunity to hold Laura and to be alone with her. Laura looked so sweet and so peaceful. We cried, kissed her still-warm forehead, and asked that she now pray for us. I never thought to ask the nurse's name, but I still offer a prayer of thanks for her understanding.

The ride from the hospital back to Ellen's seemed never to end. But we got there. We leaned on each other. The phone kept ringing and the blur continued. Ellen's family was coming. Judi was flying in from Illinois. Other siblings of Ellen and Fred somehow got there. It was 11:00 a.m. now and getting harder to focus on anything.

I wished I could ease the pain reflected on Ellen's face. My husband's eyes were vacant. Ellen's parents looked pained. People spoke to me and I think I spoke back. I remember that it was 4:00 p.m. We would have to leave for the airport soon.

The entire family started out to meet Fred at the airport. It was decided that Fred's dad, Ellen, and the girls would go to the plane to meet him while the rest of us stayed in the private room given to us by the airport personnel.

My husband later told me that Fred's first words were, "Where's Laura?" When Fred came into the room where we were, he seemed to be in a trance. What could any of us say? We simply hugged.

Family members supported each other that night. It was another blur. We ate what was supposed to be party food. I can't recall any conversations. We all just "were." We only said what had to be said, but I felt close to the others in the sometimes-stark silence. We were grieving. I went down to the basement to wash some clothes. It seemed important to just do something. Nothing else made sense.

All I could think about was how angry I was at God. How could He do such a thing? What cruelty. What an untimely thing for Him to do. My angry feelings continued throughout the sadness of the following day. I hollered and screamed at God under my breath.

The continuing blur makes it hard to remember the sequence of events. I remember ironing Laura's dress at some point. My husband and I and Ellen's parents went to choose the tiny white casket. I remember being in a flower shop. Somehow we functioned in that blur. Somehow we were at the funeral home the next day. Friends were coming and going.

I hugged Fred and sat him down to talk. I shared my anger at God with my son. I went on and on about how God's timing was incredibly bad. "How could He do this? What timing. On the day you come home. At 5:00 yesterday morning you spoke with your wife and thanked God for your homecoming, and at 5:00 that same afternoon you came home to be told your daughter had died."

His response was simple. "No Mom, God's timing was good. What if God had taken Laura when I was away? I might not have been able to get back quickly. He waited until I was on my way. He wanted Laura but he took care of Ellen and the girls. I thank Him for that." His eyes were so sad. He hugged me.

I breathed deeply. He was right. Fred's faith helped me to lean on rather than to yell at God.

The sounds of the other children stirring upstairs brought me out of the memory trance. Little Freddy was still asleep on my shoulder. Somehow I knew that Laura knew my thoughts and that she was prayerfully smiling at God's gifts to us.

I thank God for my son's faith that allowed me to begin the healing that will never be complete—but becomes more tolerable as time goes by.

I thank God for family members. Together we weathered a storm that brought me closer to those with whom I could pour out my heart, yell at, become irritated with, pray with, grieve with, and, finally, lean on. God gave us family to love. Laura magnified that love. Laura taught us how important each of us is. Laura reminded us that love is giving—one to the other.

I often remind our other grandchildren that they have a cousin in heaven to pray for them. I feel Laura's presence often, especially at family functions. I felt her presence when her brother Freddy was born. I felt her there at the birth of her youngest cousin two months later.

Yes! Laura is around me a lot. Forget Laura? Never. And Laura hasn't forgotten us. Laura's gift is precious. She taught us all how strong love is and how love transcends life on earth.

ROSEMARIE GORTLER, a Licensed Professional Counselor, is also a freelance writer. She is the co-author of a seven-volume religious book series for children, published by Our Sunday Visitor. *The Ten Commandments for Children*, the fourth in the series, was a second-place award winner from the Catholic Press Association of the United States and Canada. Ms. Gortler has also had several articles published in the *St. Anthony Messenger* and other magazines.

John Russell Ore in 1990

FIXING DEATH

BY NANCY BAUER-KING

October 6, 1990

"Goodbye, John. Goodbye, John," Becky and Bobby call. My grandchildren are lying on their tummies next to the open grave and throwing cut flowers from funeral bouquets onto the casket of their 16-month-old brother.

Charlie, my husband of six months, is lying next to them and helping the two preschoolers give these farewell gifts to John. I'm standing several yards away watching the sunlight bathe my former in-laws. They are bunched underneath a maple tree with leaves that shimmer in full fall yellow and gold brilliance. They are angry with my son, Steve, for the break-up of his marriage to John's mother, Jane. Even now they stand at a distance.

The short, stocky priest, who has ignored mentioning Steve's name throughout the funeral, has intoned his magic incantations and is gone. Other friends and family members, still shaken by the little boy's sudden death three days earlier, are slowly winding their way through rows of headstones toward their cars.

The mourners, who are walking into the autumn afternoon, have heard two very different accounts of the tragedy.

Jane tells people her son died of SIDS. Steve describes a different scene.

"John had been sick," Steve says, "and was having difficulty breathing Tuesday night. Jane made a doctor's appointment for Wednesday morning, and I went to the house to go to the doctor with them.

"Jane met me at the door and told me she couldn't get John to sleep last night. That he just kept fussing, so she finally just shut his bedroom door. She said she could still hear his labored breathing through the door when she went to bed.

"I thought—oh, no! I dreaded what I was going to find." Steve's job as a fireman and paramedic had led him through doors into dozens of horrible scenes, but none like this.

"I knew he was dead when I saw him, but I tried to revive him," Steve cried. "The little guy had put up a fight. I had to peel his fingers off the crib.

"Jane says he died of SIDS, but I met with the doctor. And the death certificate says epiglottitis."

I knew that some nasty bug had attacked John so that he couldn't breathe, but Steve had to give me an anatomy lesson. He described the epiglottis, an elastic flap of cartilage that keeps food from going into the windpipe. Steve said the disease had caused the tissue to become swollen and cut off John's air.

Steve's story implied that Jane's decisions contributed to the terrible consequence. Already in process, their divorce was final a few months after the funeral, and the two stories took their places among the other furnishings of the two divided households.

At age 50, I had experienced a number of deaths and thought I knew how to manage grief. I did all the right things. Cried. Talked. Journaled. All at appropriate times. But the scene that Steve described kept flashing through my head while reading the newspaper, driving to the grocery store, making love with Charlie.

And in the weeks following John's funeral, my grief began to affect my work as the pastor of two United Methodist churches. "The people are saying you are taking too long to get over your grandson's death," my district superintendent told me in November after a church meeting.

I sought counseling when I could not control the intrusion of that mental image of *my* son giving John mouth-to-mouth respiration in a futile attempt to save his *dead* son.

I described to the counselor the circumstances of John's death, the shredded family relationships, the effect my grief was having on the congregations I serve, and the two stories.

I rationalized my former daughter-in-law's behavior.

"I understand Jane's version of the events," I said. "I can't think of anything worse than losing a child. And to bear some responsibility would be a special horror. Denial must be one option for her."

"Can you talk with her?" my counselor asked.

"No."

"Why not?"

"She's going for sole custody of their other two children," I answered. "And I want to support my son."

"Ah," said the counselor and then added, "Isn't soul custody what you do?" She saw my confusion and added, "You know, custody of souls."

I grinned at her quip and thought of all the deaths I had attended, all the family stories I had heard, and all the good people trying to make meaning out of their suffering.

"So, how is *your* soul?" the counselor asked.

"I'm scared," I said.

"One of the scenes of John's death."

"Yes?" The counselor prompted.

"I'm afraid to look at it."

"What do you think would happen if you looked."

"I would collapse. Lose complete control. Never quit sobbing."

She listened carefully and then said, "You know, when one looks directly into the center of pain, it always changes." And after I learned to trust her, I allowed her to lead me mentally into John's bedroom.

I watch my former daughter-in-law grip the doorknob as my son quickly pries tiny fingers from wooden slats, lifts his baby boy from the crib, places him on the floor, and leans over a limp body.

I cried and cried. And then stopped.

I am surprised that the scene has changed. Less pain. Less intense.

"What are you feeling?" the counselor asked as I handed her back her box of Kleenex.

"I can't fix it!" I said. "I want to fix it and I can't."

"Kind of an occupational hazard, isn't it?" she asked.

I nodded and said, "Yes. Clergy talk about their Messiah complex. I tell folks I can't fix it, but I really want to try."

October 6, 2011

Twenty-one years have passed. For 21 years, the two stories of John's death seemed to lie buried in family history. Then, suddenly, a few weeks ago, after an argument between my son Steve and his son Bobby, the stories of John's death came back to life.

An altercation over financial responsibility had been brewing between Steve and Bobby for a few months. In an escalation of the conflict, Bobby, now 24, sent Steve a brief text message. *You just lost another son,* Bobby typed and cut off all contact with his dad.

Steve's account of the argument included a story of disagreement over bills, living arrangements, and care of a pet. I have not heard my grandson's version, but his typed proclamation to Steve indicates a deep grief about his little brother's death. A sleeping grief that was awakened when Bobby experienced an unrelated hurt and anger.

I would like to fix the fallout from John's death that has surfaced between Steve and Bobby. I can't. I can't fix my former daughter-in-law's take on reality or the discrepancy between the two stories being spun about the terrible tragedy.

And I can't fix the hurt between my son and grandson, or the stories they believe about their disagreement. I can love them both. I can be in touch with each of them and I can listen. But I can't fix it.

However, I *can* tell my own stories. I can describe the scenes surrounding John's death that are fixed in my memory, some faded, some changed through the repetitive telling to loved ones.

And I can attest to the staying power of grief.

Referring to the pain she was feeling shortly after her son committed suicide, a woman I know cried to her sister, "Does this ever go away?"

"No," replied the sister, who also had a son who had killed himself years before. "It lessens, but I think about him every day."

John died 21 years ago, and family members are still winding their way through painful, contradictory, and unresolved stories about his death.

As the matriarch now, I find myself keeper of the stories of my ancestors. But what about the generations to follow? What stories do Becky and Bobby believe about their brother's death? Do they remember throwing flowers into his grave? Do they remember their "Goodbye, John, Goodbye."

And what stories are being told about the rift between Steve and Bobby?

I once heard Maya Angelou give the keynote address at a conference on writing. "You must tell the story true," she said, then added, "It takes courage, but deep down we know the truth, and 'the truth will set us free.'"

I remembered an old poster that depicted a rag doll pulled halfway through the ringer of a washing machine. The slogan:

The truth will *set you free, but first it will make you miserable.*

But Angelou is correct. I am 71 years old and have been a character in several tragic stories. Though it hurts, I have learned that looking straight into the truth will help "fix" my suffering.

Someone said, "Death steals everything except our stories." Now in her 70s, **Nancy Bauer King** wants to bequeath stories that honor the many characters in her life who nurtured her and helped her to grow into a grateful old woman. Born and raised in southern Wisconsin, she enjoys writing, reading, and gatherings with family and friends. Both Nancy and her husband Charles are retired United Methodist pastors and live in Racine, Wisconsin. They have hundreds of stories and will spin them to anyone with the patience to listen.

The poplar stump

"A windstorm blew over the top half of my poplar tree friend. The city decided it was too dangerous as a half tree, so they cut it down to a stump."

THE STUMP

By Jane Pawson

Claudia Pawson was my mother. She was an amazing woman. Born in 1918, she was the only girl in a family of three boys and the second oldest. She had an "Oh, yeah" attitude. She loved fun and made friends instantly. She was a looker and kept up with the latest fashions. (Mod was the last one she really embraced in a big way.) She got herself through the Depression and World War II like so many of that remarkable Victory generation. She met my dad after the war and was all ready to embrace family and the new hope and prosperity of the era. Mom was tough; she never seemed to catch colds, she survived two bouts of lung cancer that should have killed her and could out-dig me in the garden any day. I had the honor to live with her the last 16 years of her life.

Mair Smith was my dear friend and mentor. Mair was a living example of spirit, change and transformation. She had been born in England just before World War II. She spent the war in Ireland, doted upon by her mother and grandmother. She told me she was totally unaware of the horror going on in Europe since she was surrounded by this strong maternal love and beautiful enchanted Irish garden.

Mair studied and became a home economics teacher and married and had two children. She and her family immigrated to Canada, I think in the '70s. Then something big happened in Mair's life. Her marriage ended and she came out as a lesbian. I met her in the early '80s at a goddess circle. By then, no one could ever tell she'd been a home economics teacher.

She was one of the feminist innovators in our city. She started the first "womyn's" bookstore here, and worked on many women's rights groups. She brought sacred circle dancing to Edmonton as well as many other spiritual events. Mair was a community builder extraordinaire. She was enamored with communications and all things computers, especially Apple. She went to Findhorn—an intentional community in Scotland—a few times and became a transformation game facilitator. She brought many workshops of all types to Edmonton on faith in the universe alone. She would loan me books, and we'd talk of the cosmos together. She was my cure for depression.

Then Mair found a lump in her breast. She did the surgery and treatments like it was no biggie. Then there was another positive test and then a third. She even did death differently. She was eager for the next adventure on the other side. In her palliative care room, she set the tone to let it be a place full of joy. Even the nurses commented.

My mother died of a stroke at age 91 on July 10, 2010, the day before Mair's memorial. It was 20 days after Mair had died. I was too exhausted to go to Alberta Beach for Mair's life celebration. I had three weeks of hospital visiting and three days of death vigil and had missed mom's passing by 15 minutes. I regret that, but there was no way I could scrape myself together. I sent a clay labyrinth plaque in my stead. I know she would have loved that. The plaque became the centre of the memorial circle at the celebration.

I had a tree friend in Millcreek Ravine. I watched it grow for 50-some years. It had become a huge, majestic black poplar. It had survived ravine fires, storms, and even a lightening strike. Then, a year before Mom and Mair died, a windstorm blew over the top half of my poplar tree friend. The city decided it was too dangerous as a half tree, so they cut it down to a stump. I walked by that stump everyday on my way home from work. I'd watch the wood dry out and turn grey. I'd still pat it and say hi, though it was gone.

Not long after Mom and Mair passed, I took some time off from work to grieve. My regular walks by the tree were disrupted. A month later I went back to work and walked by my tree friend's stump, and there were shoots of new saplings in two distinct groups. Rising up from the seemingly dead wood of the stump, one group of saplings for Mair and one group for Mom. It felt like Mom and Mair giving me some sort of confirmation of hope and rebirth in all cycles of seasons and life and death.

JANE PAWSON lives in Edmonton, Alberta and is an ardent nature lover. She has been fascinated in the mysteries surrounding death and renewal since childhood.

Beth's eighth grade graduation, with her brother Doug on the left,
her father Malcolm Thomas Stephenson on the right.

"The death of my dad was a strange and beautiful gift.
At 15, I began to see my life differently. It has been a slow understanding,
for it had to go to the roots."

SPROUTING: A JOURNEY OF TRANSFORMATION

BY BETH WALKER STEPHENSON

How could I know that on December 13, 1978, when I was 15, my life would change so radically? I was in that state between dreams, tasting the last sweet morsels of cocoon-like sleep before my alarm would awaken me to the day. I heard a knock, and my mom opened my door. Her eyes were filled with tears. All I remember her saying was, "Dad has been taken to the hospital in an ambulance."

Yet as she closed the door, the room filled with a light and love that I had not seen or felt in this lifetime, but bone-deep, I remember. It was in every breath, every pore from which my skin rose in welcoming. It was as if I were the one being taken home. But it was not my time, it was my dad's.

I was swept up in arms lighter than air, stronger than death. He was there, his essence, everything that he was and more. In this light, there was no sadness, or separation, just pure love. No want or need, just being. So this was death? How could this be? This was pure ecstasy! Everything made sense; it was as if the whole of his life experience, and mine up to this point, multiplied itself over in understanding; a millefleured new entity seemed to be formed. We were in the arms of the Great Love, and we were one.

I don't know how long this experience lasted, but the feel of it is still with me. Over 34 years I have digested it, worn it close, rubbed it smooth like a favorite stone. The wisdom that was shared planted a seed in me. The death of my dad was a strange and beautiful gift. At 15, I began to see my life differently. It has been a slow understanding, for it had to go to the roots.

At the time, a chasm separated the Light from the human side of this great loss. Death had to manifest itself in the mundane. At first, I was shocked to see my dad's body in a casket at the funeral home, his skin cold and lifeless, smelling of embalming fluid and funereal makeup. But this was not really him. This was his earthly shell, his earth suit, and he had shed it only hours ago. How could my dad be so alive and vibrant and hugging me just moments ago, and now lie here like a wax replica in a museum? This was the hardest reality shift. How could I make sense of this? What had happened to me in my room was way more real than this, and yet I could touch him here and know this was his body. But yesterday morning, I had touched his soul.

After attending both the visitation and the funeral, connecting with dear friends and family that came great distances, and the lovely, bear-like embraces that are so characteristic of the men in my family, I was filled up with their love for the moment. That morning, I was taught by my dad that the hugs were essential, and to take each one, for they held a merging of Spirit that would help sustain me through this. But this bolstering was temporary, and soon afterward I was left feeling hollow. It felt physical, this loss. This great man, this lovely, affectionate, twinkling-eyed father was gone.

The experience of loss became a hole, "the vacuous black hole" I called it, and it took years to get me to face it. After I broke up with my long-term boyfriend in college, the death hit me double hard. I went through my own kind of death, wearing black, deep, kohl-rimmed eyes, staying up until the wee hours, and sleeping until late afternoon. Sylvia Plath's books strewn across my floor that I had poured feverishly through became the bricks of my entombment. I numbed myself with herb and sleep. I flunked out of school and sank into the black pit. I moved back in with my mom, into my old room, which I called the "womb tomb." How could I fit into this space after so much change? The blue-and green-flowered wallpaper and deep, blue-green shag carpeting were a constant reminder of what I was not and could not be any more. I was still so much a child at 20, still empty, longing for peace.

It was as if I had to nearly die in order to really live. My rebirth is a bit of a mystery to me to this day. I met a lot of caring beautiful people with whom I could connect, and they began to help mend my tender places. Psychedelic experiences put me in touch again with my child-self. I saw things with the wonder that I remembered as a young child. I shared life anew! This opened a pinhole of understanding. I realized I had all I needed or wanted inside me. I wrote vast volumes on lineless paper, which piled up high in corners of my room. I reconnected with a special friend from childhood who was a good listener, and we shared comforting Bible passages, which grounded me. I am forever grateful for the time Gillian shared with me. She was such an important piece of bringing the shattered fragments of my self back to wholeness.

I sought counseling with a man named Dr. Gandhi, strangely enough! He had such soulful eyes, and I knew he was very wise. I shared my story of Dad's death with him, and he told me that he, too, had experienced something very similar with his grandmother who lived in India. He was in the States, and one moment he saw her face, surrounded in light, and the words going through his head and heart were, "I'll always be with you."

This was what was spiraling around in me since my encounter with my dad right after his death! This was an epiphany for me. Up until now, I had not met or heard of anyone who had my experience. It had remained an enigma, and something I could not name. I even at times doubted that it ever happened.

After meeting Dr. Gandhi, things began to make sense for me. I read many books that a later counselor, Cook Rollo, gave me. I began to run again. I felt like a newborn. Lighter, freer, tender, and unfettered.

Another important element woven throughout this experience was the relationship with my best friend and long love, Steve. I met him in my early teens. My dad had even pointed out that I needed to come back to church because the new pastor had a son my age who was cute. That sure got eye rolls from me! Interestingly enough, I did start to get involved in the youth choir and youth group, and decided on my own that Steve was definitely worth getting to know. He was intelligent and kind, and a bit of a mystery, which I always loved. He was shy, and that really intrigued me.

We got to know each other first as friends, and then things blossomed. We were a good combination. There was a lot of laughter and fun in our relationship, and a lot to ponder. Our families had similar faith backgrounds and values, which helped a great deal. He was the slower, more deliberate, grounded guy who was a good anchor to my impetuous nature. I was his spice; we were each other's entertainment. At 14, I was so in love. I knew I had met the guy I was going to marry. It was just a known for us, though others doubted. At the time my dad died, I was in a very good space. I was in love, and everything felt right with my world.

In the following months, Dad's death deeply affected every aspect of my life. It shook me to the roots. I remember wondering how I could ever be happy again. I felt numb, out of touch, and uncertain about all the aspects of my life that, before the death, were givens. It took many years of journaling, conversations, dreams, and visions before I could feel like myself again. It was a hellish, dark journey that I equated to what a plant must feel pushing up out of the earth between cracks in a sidewalk. I hope never to go so deeply into such a dark place again. In retrospect, I now know that I was not alone, but I often could not feel the loving guidance and understanding from others during that period of time I was cocooned. I eventually made it, and was stronger, more resilient, and, ultimately, deeply happier. It was then that I learned that I could rely just on myself. This is something that I would never wish on myself, or anyone else ever, but I could do it.

There have been times I needed to connect with my dad. Most of the time, I have switched to my mom, in the land of the living. However, there was an experience when I was around 21 and broken up with Steve for approximately a year. I was living with a dear friend in her room, and there were 11 other women living in the home. She was going to school full time and working, and I had recently had a rather challenging situation present itself. Her boyfriend one evening told me point blankly that I needed to leave, right then. I had other friends, but this was quite sudden, and I hadn't had any time to come to terms with it, or even find a place to stay. Within five minutes' time, a good friend stopped by the room, and handed me a key to his place.

I stayed there, sharing the only bed in the apartment with him. I was in a bad state. I was anxious and fretful, and I didn't feel grounded. The incident just added to the unrest that I was feeling inside. I am surprised I eventually got to sleep that night. Then I had an experience unlike any other. I don't know if I dreamed it, or traveled in my sleep, but it felt real. I was flying through space and time when I saw what seemed to be an angelic, winged shape in the distance, on a place that seemed like the dark side of the moon. As I approached, I saw that the being was full of light, and it wrapped its arms around me. The memory is vague, but the experience was profound. A deep healing that took place during my sleep. I awoke, staring into the eyes of my friend, his eyes as wide as mine. I said not a word. He said, "It really happened, I was there!"

My mom has shared that sometimes life is stranger than fiction, and in that moment, I knew she was right. I think it was the love energy of my father that wrapped itself around my wounded self and comforted me like a child. This experience altered my understanding of the power of love to transcend death. It instilled in me the knowing that there really isn't any such thing as death. As I got up and started my day, the old anxiety was completely gone, and I was whole once more.

I felt as if I had spent an indeterminate time in the darkness, thinking, incubating, waiting. Ultimately I felt I was the co-creator of my new self. I grew to love what I have become. My dad used to say, "Out of the shit rise beautiful flowers!" Indeed.

My intuition was stronger in the aftermath of my dad's death. My gift became more finely tuned. Ultimately what changed was my paying attention. There is so much happening all around us all of the time, both inwardly and in the outside world. When I began to slow down and keep moving my focus back to the here and now, I found that my anxiety about the future, and concerns about the past, ceased to exist. Over the years, this practicing being in the present has expanded to the point where more often I feel a deep abiding joy about my life. I have goals for the future and have reconciled with the past. The present is full enough on its own, and I am now comfortable in my own skin, even ecstatic at times.

I have come to realize that every single moment that I am alive is precious. I can step outside of my own judgment of myself and therefore forgive and let others live their lives. Everyone is growing at their own rate with their own issues, and it is all perfect. Of course, occasionally I will step back into the role of using unkind thoughts about myself, but I acknowledge this much more quickly. It is being mindful and awake that brings me back to center.

I received a profound blessing through the loss of my dad at a young age. What has taken most people their whole lives I have been able to understand years sooner. I believe this gift was given for a reason. It has given me insight into others' lives. It has helped me to be mostly free of the self-imposed bondage of thoughts that had enslaved my thinking. In essence, his death caused me to wake up. To appreciate fully the gift of life. To embrace fully every new experience, and to challenge myself to grow toward a fuller understanding.

Where this will lead me in the years to come I can only guess, but I know, as my dad told me on the morning of his death that he will always be with me. This is even encoded on my fingertips as I type. For years, when I first touched the keys, they would instantly want to type out, "today and every day for the rest of your life." Until that time I can stand in full embrace with him once again, I know I am being held, in arms that hold the understanding of Love.

BETH WALKER STEPHENSON lives in the Driftless region, in Viroqua, Wisconsin. She has been with her husband Steve for 35 years. She has two children, Jonah 19, and Isabella, 11. She attended Illinois Wesleyan University and graduated from Illinois State University in English and Parks and Recreation Administration. She loves to hike, bike, paddle, dance, sing, and write poetry and short stories, and is putting the finishing touches on a young adult fictional tale.

"Pablo was pure boy—all trucks, trains, hoses,
sprinklers, pumps and puddles."

THE SWEETEST HEART
ELLEN HOLTY

In the summer of 2007, we left northern California for the high desert of Taos, New Mexico, thinking life would be cheaper and we could enjoy winters outdoors. My husband, Javier, and I had three kids under the age of six: Luna was five, Pablo was three, and Mercy was one. They call those the "blurly" years. I had my hands full. Luna was precocious and domineering, Pablo was sunny and caring, and Mercy was the dancing, goofy hug machine. That fall Javier started teaching first grade at the small, private Waldorf school in town.

Our new house was a dream come true, as was the yard, with a swing set and a play house, cacti, evergreens, chamisa, sage, fruit trees and irises. The girls and I planted bulbs and seeds while Pablo investigated the elaborate irrigation system. He was pure boy—all trucks, trains, hoses, sprinklers, pumps and puddles. He had a thing for water. He reminded everyone of their sons at his age. My mom remembers watching him at a playground as he circled the entire place, checking everything out before stopping near some boys digging a ditch. He stood there until one of them asked if he wanted a shovel. He nodded and joined them. He was a gentleman.

Early in the school year, Pablo started acting strangely. I was unloading a box from the van when he screamed that HE wanted to bring the box to the house. His insistence was totally unlike him. Unable to talk him out of it, I took the box back to the van, and together we carried it back to the house. But, whatever? He was three. Three-year-olds are wacky. It was his first time in school. Transitions are hard.

I decided to build him a ship in the back yard with found lumber and a drill. I painted a light blue bird on the side and put tree stumps inside for seats. He wasn't into it, but I thought the hammering and painting might encourage him to be creative. I hung wind chimes on one of the beams and screwed an

145

old ceiling fan onto the mast for kinetic interest. I wanted him to know I was trying to help him.

Soon he was getting compulsive about all sorts of things. He insisted on being the only person to open and close the garage door. He had to get out of the van before anyone else or he would scream. Whenever I put new groceries into the refrigerator, he took them out, put them back on the counter, and put them in the fridge himself. That was extra nerve wracking, especially with eggs, when he wobbled and knocked into things. He ran into doorknobs. Three days in a row he fell down, hitting on the exact same spot on his forehead. He seemed half asleep all the time.

The doctor said he was a normal three-year-old. Kids fall down. Kids play with their spit. Kids scratch their friends. Not *my* kid! Pablo was an extremely gentle boy. We took him to a homeopath and a medicine man, whom he scratched quite badly. He didn't want anyone talking about him or touching him. One day he took a nap, which he hadn't done in at least a year, and slept for three hours. When he woke up, his eyes drooped and his mouth contorted into a hideous grimace. That's when I knew in my heart that my beloved boy was leaving us.

A second doctor scheduled a CAT scan for the following week. In the parking lot of the insurance provider's office, I opened the side door of the van and Pablo fell out onto his head. He got up, said, "That didn't hurt," and staggered away. I was panicking, in tears, trying to herd him and 18-month-old Mercy into the building.

The scan revealed what our doctor had suspected: a mass in his brain. After much searching on the Internet, I had concluded that a removable brain tumor was our best hope, and remained hopeful that the "glioma" would be operable. He was immediately booked at the University of New Mexico hospital in Albuquerque, three hours away, for that night. The whole family loaded into the van and headed south.

The Special Pediatrics Ward was brand new and well equipped. The staff took good care of Pablo and various philanthropic groups showered him with gifts. In the playroom, I chased after his rolling IV stand while he made Legos bounce around in a little blender. The vibe in our room and on the whole ward was somber. I asked a nurse if anybody got out of there alive. "Some do," she said, and returned to the papers on her desk. Mostly Pablo wanted me to read to him or he wanted to be in the bathtub, playing with the infinitely entertaining hand-held shower head.

The next day, Pablo was seen by the pediatric oncologist, the nutritionist, the neurologist, and the social worker. They were somber, too. That night, while trying to sleep before Pablo's 4 a.m. MRI, I wondered if I was coming down with something. Even covered with several heated blankets, lying next to Pablo in his hospital bed, I couldn't get warm. And I couldn't fill my lungs with air. And I couldn't eat anything. I asked one nurse if I might have pneumonia. After hearing my symptoms, she said, "No. It's classic anxiety. I know, because I have the same thing." And she got me a chocolate Boost—the first of many protein drinks that kept me alive there. Later that day, Thanksgiving, we got the results of the scan.

Pablo's small room was full of all the people who'd worked with him over the previous 48 hours and others I didn't recognize, maybe 15 in all. Most of them fidgeted or appeared to be on the verge of tears. The oncologist handed me a Neurology for Kids handout that wasn't supposed to make me feel like an idiot; it was just the best resource she could find for explaining what was going on in my son's brain. Then she got down to it. He had a five-centimeter diffuse intrinsic pontine glioma, which is a large tumor spread throughout the brain stem. Even a biopsy would threaten his very basic functions—respiration, digestion, everything. It was inoperable. And terminal.

"But there isn't nothing we can do," she said. He could have radiation, and was welcome to stay in the hospital. I didn't understand. Why give him radiation if he were terminal? Why put him through agony so he might feel better for a while, then make him die longer?

"I like to be hopeful," the radiologist said.

"Have you ever cured anyone of this?" I asked.

"No," he said. "But I read about it once."

I looked at my husband and said, "I want to bring him home."

The oncologist was taken aback a second, but looked me in the eye and said quietly, "I don't blame you."

I staggered through a labyrinth of hallways and elevators and lobbies and stairs before I reached the exit, snow falling, people walking in and out as I screamed *WHY?* from the pit of my being. I wailed and sobbed and roared. Some guy cautiously asked if I was okay, like I'd escaped from the psycho ward.

I was scared that I was hyperventilating and did the only thing I knew to calm myself down—some basic yoga: a sun salutation. As all that anxiety dispersed through my body, at last I could breathe. I couldn't stop weeping, but at least I could breathe.

We soon left for home, the five of us back in the van, shaken and changed. It was not a smooth transition. The heating in our house wasn't working, and we had no hot water. Immediately our plight brought us help from our new community and things were fixed and handled and provided. The outpouring of love from these new friends was incredible.

A dad from the school delivered a half cord of firewood he'd cut. All the seventh and eighth grade students from the Waldorf school came to our house and sang for our family one morning. A neighbor I didn't know very well asked if she could take out my recycling every few days on her way to drop off hers. People gave us flower essences, artwork, toys for the kids, bags of groceries, meals, and books. One great gift for me came from a friend who researched all the alternative therapies she could find on the Internet and then boiled them down to a few remote possibilities. That was invaluable because we wanted to make sure we weren't overlooking any options, but there was no way I was going to spend my remaining days with my son staring at a computer. Another friend, a physician, spent a day researching Pablo's illness and assured us that all the kids, 300 a year, who have this kind of tumor die. We felt supported and certain in our decision to bring Pablo home.

Our hospice nurse, Cathy, was a lifeline, a crucial link to the medical world as we worked out how best to care for Pablo ourselves. She was in contact with Pablo's UNM doctors and brought his prescriptions. She always made time to discuss our impossible questions. I just wanted to know what to expect, what Pablo was going to have to go through, what I was going to have to see. Of course she couldn't tell me exactly, but she always had a pretty good idea of what the coming week would look like.

In my efforts to make Pablo's final days as beautiful, natural, and painless as possible, Cathy was an expert collaborator. I wanted Pablo to remain as coherent as possible, without excessive medications that might prolong his suffering. He was on two main oral meds, dexamethasone, a steroid to contain the swelling of the tumor, and Ativan, for agitation. The steroid was the drug I had the most problems with, as it made Pablo so hungry he actually got pudgy.

It didn't seem right that my dying child was eating several times in the middle of the night and gaining weight. The tumor, however, was impinging on his cranial nerves, and could at any moment start compromising one of his basic brain stem functions. Cathy and I worked constantly to get Pablo's dosage just right. She was a gifted nurse and became a dear friend.

Within days, the three Waldorf schools where Javier had worked mobilized for us—the San Francisco Waldorf High School, Summerfield Waldorf School & Farm, and the Taos Waldorf School. The San Francisco school prayed for us at assemblies and gave us end-of-life wisdom, Summerfield sent innumerable packages and two dear Early Childhood teacher friends to visit us, and the Taos school was our daily support. Teachers at each of these schools shared Pablo's story with their students with honesty and wonder, inviting the children to participate in the mystery of dying. One friend from Summerfield asked his students to draw a picture of what they would eat if they could eat anything in the world and sent us a stack of hilarious drawings. His class also sent Pablo a wooden sword they'd all blessed and signed. Students in Taos painted prayer flags that we strung around our house and yard, like garlands of friends. One family from Summerfield made an Advent calendar out of walnut shells with beautiful beads inside each one. It was so magical! With so much love, my spirits were kept up every day. I believe people actually relieved my suffering with their actions. I floated on a raft of prayers and sweetness.

I needed it. For the first few weeks we were home, Pablo only wanted to be with Javier. All I wanted to do was to hold and comfort my boy, and he would push me away and say, "I want Dada!" It was hard to stay positive through that. I knew that Pablo and his dad were doing their work of letting go together, but I was terrified that he would die without me ever holding him again.

In those early weeks Pablo wanted to go on adventures with his dad. His favorite thing to do was go to the airport to watch planes and helicopters take off and land. He didn't want to get out of the car, he just wanted to watch. Often they went to the ice rink and Javier pushed Pablo around the ice on a chair. One time Pablo got to ride on the Zamboni.

In the back of our minds, an unimaginable quandary always loomed—whether to bury or cremate our son. Everyone had opinions, and I had no strong feelings one way or another. I could barely entertain the question. Then one day a bird flew into our kitchen window and broke its neck. Doing what we always did with the dead critters we found, we dug a hole in the back yard and thanked it for its life and buried it. It was clear to me then that burial was the most relatable way for the girls to honor their brother.

So Javier, Pablo and I drove into one of the more surreal experiences of my life. At Las Cruces Cemetery, Pablo sat bundled in a blanket in the front seat while Javier and I chose a plot. *It's inconceivable, the idea of putting him in the ground, this boy, who now, right here, is alive, with me, eating an ice cream sandwich, dying. How? What was he going to be? Where was he going to go, the alive part, his life? How do you bury your child?*

At those times I turned to Pema Chodron. Her book *The Places That Scare You* was all I read while Pablo was sick. She writes about using our suffering to feel compassion for others who are suffering too. She also reminded me to stay in the present moment. It was the only safe place to be—the past full of guilt and blame, the future full of dread. And at that moment in the cemetery, Pablo was alive, and I was alive, and I needed to breathe and listen and feel the ground under my feet and the cold on my cheeks. One moment following another.

Javier made the arrangements for the plot. I focused on my daily job, which was feeding everyone and taking care of the girls as best I could. Luna was not taking it well, but Mercy, just a toddler, danced and waved at everyone, seeming to have enough joy for the whole world. Around her it was hard to get too sad about anything.

I took the night shifts with Pablo, which meant reading to him or feeding him. On Christmas Eve morning, he was awake by 8, already on his second bowl of ice cream of the day. I had given him five bowls between 10pm and 2am the night before. I suggested to Cathy we decrease the steroids again, and increase the Ativan- less hunger, more sleep. I just couldn't believe he should be so hungry.

Later that day our friend Rebeca came to give us massages. Pablo wanted one, too, so he lay on his dad's chest while she massaged him. It was a sacred connection for us all. After a half an hour working with Luna, Rebeca was amazed that she couldn't help Luna release any of the palpable tension in her body. Luna was an enigma. I couldn't get through to her either.

That December we hosted Advent gatherings on Sunday nights. Pablo usually sat on the living room sofa with Javier or listened to Luna's kindergarten teacher, Silke, tell the kids a story or play the guitar. On Christmas Eve, while a small group of friends ate and talked and sang in front of the fire, Pablo climbed on my lap while I gave gifts to our friends. He fell asleep on my shoulder as tears filled my eyes. I hadn't held him in so long. I was so grateful to feel him again, peaceful and warm in my arms.

Christmas day, however, was very difficult. Despite the love and gifts of family and friends, despair hung heavily on our home.

That night, Pablo slept better, but not soundly. He still showed no symptoms since decreasing the steroids. In general he was calm and not in pain. He laughed at "bushy-backed sea slug" in *Harry By the Sea*. Everyone got a kick out of hearing him laugh, and we kept repeating it, wanting to hear him laugh again and again. From my journal a few days after Christmas:

And Pablo? What will I want from these pages? To feel him alive again? A glimpse, a physical memory, sparked by language, a sensory impulse?

He doesn't want to wear clothes anymore, so when we snuggle I can nuzzle his beautiful smooth skin on his shoulder, his arm, his left arm pit. There's a beautiful soft warm spot around his temple and hairline I kiss whenever I can. His feet are dry and cracking almost, his hands, too.

Today I pretended my name was Roxanne and I was serving him at a restaurant. "Where are you from?" I asked. "Africa," he said, without missing a beat. And I was shocked, really, at how alive his imagination is, and how little I've played with him. When I asked him how old he was, he showed me his last three fingers, then tried to make a half with another one. "Three and a half," he said. Such a sweet, innocent soul, untainted, forgiving, otherworldly, angelic.

The next two weeks I spent 24/7 with Pablo. He was no longer walking, and his left hand started curling in toward his body. I carried him to the kitchen to get his food. I carried him in the shower, too. My right bicep was enormous. One afternoon as he napped, he twitched and mumbled—without pain or distress—as if the tumor were spreading neuron by neuron throughout his body. He was peaceful, so I just watched, practicing letting go of him. Day by day, as he slowly departed, he ate less and drank more fluids.

His bright eyes were growing dim, but occasionally they got real wide and clear when he had an idea to share. Several times he told me we needed to plant some corn in the back yard. Once he said, "I never saw a helicopter land in the snow with skis on." One day he said he was going to fix the toilet.

Most of the time I was gushing with love for him. It flowed best when I got a lot of sleep and a few breaks. His laugh was like a stuttery wail, and he had a slight, crooked smile. The left side of his face barely moved at all, yet he was still so beautiful, just in a disfigured way. Both of his eyes splayed outward and his eyelashes seemed longer than ever. When Pablo flung himself off the bed and flailed helplessly on the floor, I would feel a momentary horror, then humor would wash over me and I'd smile at my kooky boy, pick him up, toss him back on the bed, nuzzle his cheeks, and move on.

But sometimes I felt trapped in a tedious process of suffering and demands. Often Pablo wouldn't nap, was bored, and was in need of constant care. I didn't feel like playing, I was exhausted. But there was no other place I wanted to be. Meanwhile, gifts kept coming, keeping me grateful and connected. One day, six pints of Ben & Jerry's ice cream arrived in the mail, which was a huge treat. A group of Taos friends sewed him a pillow, covered with angels that he immediately napped on. Two Japanese exchange students rallied the entire Summerfield community to fold and send us one thousand origami cranes, symbolizing healing and peace. Another friend we didn't know very well volunteered to make a cedar casket for Pablo.

One night I had a dream, sandwiched between Pablo and Luna in my bed. I saw a horrible river of dead bodies and recognized one face as mine, sneering and still, dead. As I tried to get back into my body, I heard a video game kind of noise, like when you try to do something you can't—a tinkling "da-dum." I took stock of my sensations, and did not feel cold. I didn't feel anything. I was not scared, for my state was so pleasant—entirely without sensation in the loveliest peace. Not void, just free. I was dead! Then I woke up.

I wondered, "Will Pablo know he's dead? See his body and try to get back in? Or will someone be there to greet him and show him the way to the light?" It was so real and significant, lying there between my dying son and my firstborn. I finally got out of bed to write about it, then Mercy woke up, needing some water and a snuggle. Then Pablo woke up and barfed.

Towards the end of January, he became more and more distant, eyes fluttering a lot, quite sleepy, calm, departing. I struggled to let him go. I loved him bazonkers. He got harder to understand until he could no longer speak so I made a little sign he could point to with drawings of things he might need. But he couldn't really point to it, either. Inspired by Rudolf Steiner's book *Staying Connected*, I tried an experiment. I asked Pablo a question with my thoughts, without speaking. "How will I know you when you're gone"? And an answer came clear: "In the crows." Crows... okay. Good. So I tried another question: "What should I do with all this crazy love for you?" Another clear answer: "Give it to Dad and Luna and Mercy and everyone." Okay. I could work with that.

In those final days, we were not handling it—checks were bouncing, credit cards declined. I couldn't stop crying, got furious with Luna. I walked into the bedroom one morning and found Pablo and his dad playing. Javier was holding Pablo's hand and whacking himself with it and falling down. Pabs wasn't communicating much by then, but it was clear he was enjoying it. I left them alone.

Pablo wanted me with him that afternoon, but I couldn't stop crying. He was lying down and I was leaning over him, telling him how much I loved him and how sorry I was, wiping tears off my face, when he flung his arm weakly at me, thwapping me on the cheek. I couldn't help laughing. It was like he was saying, "Get it together, Mom! Don't flake on me now!" I said, "Pablo, you have the sweetest heart." Then his eyes got wide and clear and he pointed at my heart. "*I* do?" I said, and he nodded. My precious boy.

Two days later, as pneumonia settled into Pablo's lungs, Cathy came and told us she was going to stay the night, it was time. She gave him morphine to ease the way. At about 9 p.m. she asked how we wanted to schedule the night. I apologized and said I was so exhausted I had to go straight to sleep. I was happy to wake up whenever anyone needed me to, but I had to go to bed. I lay next to Pablo, who was breathing quickly and steadily. He was working hard, but not in pain. I kissed him goodnight and crashed.

The next thing I knew it was dark, and the big candle on the dresser was still lit. It was not quite 5 a.m. I looked over to Pablo, who was still breathing fast. "Hi sweetie," I said softly. "You're doing great. You're my big strong boy. I love you so much." A few moments later he stopped breathing, and I held my breath. Then he said, "Aaaaaahh ... " and my heart jumped—it had been so long since I'd heard his voice. He breathed quickly a few more times, stopped for a while, then once more said, "Aaaaaahh ... " His hand moved slowly toward his face, and he was gone.

I was in shock, like the bomb I had been expecting to explode just floated away. So grateful, too, that he went so peacefully, and that he woke me up to be with him. It was so quiet, it was like nothing changed. But I got the sense, too, that he was busy, shooting to the stars. I woke up Javier and Cathy. They sat with him for a while. Then Javier and I bathed him with calendula oil, wrapped him in white silk cloth, and with Silke, put him in the beautiful casket our friend made.

On a wooden table covered with a silk cloth painted by the faculty of the school, we faced Pablo toward the window overlooking Taos Mountain and the snow. Friends arrived and lit zillions of candles. The girls woke up hungry and I made French toast. A flock of pinyon jays perched outside the kitchen window. I'd never seen any in our yard before, and there were at least 20! They were the same powdery blue as the bird I'd painted on Pablo's boat out back. Outside the sparrows were jubilant in song. A magpie flew by. Then, a crow. My heart jumped. It was magical and beautiful.

We kept Pablo at home for two days while family and friends and children traveled from all over the country to be with us and say goodbye. We kept the windows in the room open and it was cold, but there was always someone laughing, crying, singing, or reading. There were times I was happy to see friends, and there were times I had to lie in my bed and ache with the new emptiness. On Sunday, February 3, we had a funeral at our house.

I still can not fathom how Javier was able to speak about Pablo so clearly at the service. He reviewed Pablo's life, from his easy birth in Santa Rosa, California, through our many moves, his love of water, the arrival of his sister, his friends, and our move to Taos. Meanwhile, Luna kept interrupting him, asking him when he was going to get her a cell phone. Javier invited anyone to place things in Pablo's casket and the children brought their drawings and toys. A friend from San Francisco had sent a clay figure she'd made, and my parents placed it next to him with wooded birds they'd carved. I kissed Pablo's cold forehead and Javier closed the casket. That's when Luna howled, finally releasing her enormous pain—everyone's enormous pain.

We sang as we carried the casket to the back of our van. The snow fell thick on the white world. All the cars slowly flowed from our driveway onto the road, and we drove along the canyon to the cemetery.

Taos Mountain was dusted with snow and foggy with cloud as we stood by the grave dug deep into the ground the day before. Friends and family, grandparents and children surrounded the pile of earth. A hand-carved wooden cross stood at one end of the hole. A Lakota Sioux friend blessed Pablo's tracks with his wing of eagle feathers and sang songs with two lovely women. The men lowered down the little casket and the children and I shoveled the soil onto it. Then all the people took their turns filling the hole back up. It felt right. I felt great joy that my boy was so loved and honored even as my heart broke open to the world.

For Pablo Forest Alvarez 2/6/04 - 2/1/08
may flights of angels sing thee to thy rest

I want to let everyone know that death can be beautiful, that we often have lots of choices about how it goes, and that we can be of enormous comfort to each other. Of course, not all diagnoses are as clear as Pablo's. And hospice may not be right for everyone. I only hope our story inspires all of us to think more creatively about dying, and the things we can *do* to provide meaning, comfort, resolution, and community when we most need it.

ELLIE HOLTY is a mother of two, sometimes three children (depending when you ask), living in Ashland, Oregon. She is a caregiver, graphic designer, hospice volunteer, and an executive assistant. She is always eager to talk to people about ways to stay connected to our departed friends on the other side.

Bill and Lois Edger on a fishing trip to Canada, June 1976. They continued to fish together in Canada until 1999 when Lois became too ill too travel. After her death, Bill traveled to Canada only twice more, the last time with his daughter Ila in 2004.

Finding My Parents

Ila Edger Dezarn

"Why can't I die?"

I put down my knitting and looked across the hospital room to my Dad. It was our eighth day of hospice, but only 48 hours before they had sent him back into a nursing home saying he was stable and "wasn't going downhill anymore." The next morning he went back to the emergency room with fatal pneumonia and was checked into the hospital's hospice wing.

How do you answer that? It was a horrible question. I went to his side. All I could do was ask if he wanted me to tell the nurse to make him "more comfortable," injecting him with a higher dose of painkillers that would ease him into sleep and out of pain, but undoubtedly shorten our time together. We exchanged "I love you," and that was our last conversation. He died a few hours later, while I was holding his hand, and my boyfriend was holding my other hand.

That was another major step in my own journey, too. At 40, I had now lost both parents in the span of five years. I had moved back to my hometown to be closer to my Mom during her final year. Our time together during my previous trips home had often been spent talking, shopping, watching sports or movies, and doing the morning crossword together. But after her illness prevented those activities, my visits were more as a caregiver. While my father took care of most of the daily tasks as she grew weaker, I was the one to wash and roll her hair and trim her toenails and try to find stories to entertain her.

After her death, my Dad was lost. I found myself urging him into projects to keep him busy and his mind occupied. We did many things together that we'd always intended to do as father and daughter, like fishing and going to movies, and even to a Civil War reenactment near his home town. As he grew weaker, I began to help him do his projects—gardening, canning, cooking, and keeping up the house. It wasn't long before illness slowed him down too much, and a trip to the hospital with pneumonia led to a nursing home, a second nursing home, another hospital visit, then hospice. It was torture for a man who was never one to rely on others or ask for help.

In all my 40 years, my parents had lived in the same small house; frugal, practical people, they never wanted more. Now I had to let it go, but first had to empty it. That was when I really began discovering my parents' life.

My mother had carefully tucked away bags full of shirt boxes, some dating from 40 years previous. There were boxes full of cards congratulating them on the birth of their baby girl. I found envelopes full of recipes clipped from newspapers. My father's workbench and garage were full of tools and fishing lures passed down from generations before. My mother's boxes of unfinished craft projects were stowed under the beds. The shed was full of canning jars waiting for the next summer's harvest. My father's gun cabinet was filled with his hunting rifles standing in a row.

Sifting through the remnants of their lives with my boyfriend, I would try to explain it all to him—how my mother clipped the recipes, but my father did most of the cooking; how our summers had been full of fresh vegetables; how the dreams of the next fishing trip to Canada kept my father going through the winter; my mother's love of crafts but her lack of patience that kept her from completing many; my father's yearly foray into the woods in search of deer.

Items were packed, sold, or thrown out. The house was cleared, cleaned, and sold. And then a strange thing started to happen.

Back at my own house, I began to notice that I had accumulated a stack of cooking magazines that were waiting to have recipes cut out and saved. My own crafting, particularly knitting, had led to an accumulation of yarn and projects that were mostly unfinished. My garage was now full of tools I had saved from my father's workbench. My boyfriend became a hunter, and took one of my father's guns on his first deer hunting excursion. He enjoys cooking, and I planted a large garden for us to have a summer filled with fresh vegetables. And the canning jars were cleaned up and filled with fresh tomatoes and green beans. The boyfriend became a fiancé, then a husband. And I have a box of cards congratulating us on our wedding.

Without noticing, all of the little things that made up my parents had become a part of me. I look everywhere in my life and see them smiling. I miss them deeply, every day, but I'm carrying forward an idea that they are still alive, just in a way I had never imagined.

ILA DEZARN lives with her husband, four cats, two dogs, two emus, and a herd of alpacas in rural Kentucky near Bardstown. She holds a BFA from Murray State University and an MA from Indiana University, and continues to use her artistic talents to reflect her past and shape her future.

Ben Shapiro at his grandson's wedding.

"At the wedding reception, my father made a very public show of grabbing the [flower] garland and setting it on his own head, a show at least as embarrassing to me as so many others had been. But the photos included a close-up of my father with the garland on his head. And a smile so big, so happy, so full of life, it forced me to smile too."

BENZ REDUX

MARILYN LEYS

There are two kinds of people in the world.

The first kind enters a party and announces, "Hi! I'm *here!*"

The second kind enters a party and announces. "Hi! *You're* here!"

This was the start of a eulogy and, being a eulogy, the point of the story was to praise our friend for being the second type.

My father, on the other hand, was emphatically the first. Embarrassingly the first. A world-class spotlight hogger.

And yet, as I listened to that eulogy, I was reminded—again—of the way that his death has all but expunged the negative side of my memories, showing me, instead, a second side to Ben Shapiro's actions.

Somewhere in the welter of old photos that moves with me from house to house, there is a portrait of my family, taken by a professional photographer. I am six; I am wearing a costume that my mother sewed for the only ballet recital I ever participated in. I am a little rosebud; my petals are crepe paper. My parents are roses, too. They wore their crepe paper dresses to a Halloween party. Where my father, in his plus-size pink-and-red tutu and rose-stem cap, probably spent the evening soliciting and basking in attention.

I was too young then to be mortified. But as I grew older and grew up, it occurred to me that other people also deserved some notice. And that's when my father's actions began to seem so wrong.

Besides being shameless about how he might look, he also used his voice to attract attention. He collected jokes and bad puns, some of them bilingual, and told them whenever an occasion arose, or he arose it.

After any given funeral, when friends gathered at the home of the bereaved, he would make himself the center of the crowd, joking and quipping, insistent that even the closest relatives pay him with a smile.

No one else carried on this way, which only added to my discomfort.

He had a habit of blurting out questions, sometimes embarrassing questions, to complete strangers as well as to friends. If somebody looked foreign, he'd ask how to say "please" and "thank you" in his language. "I'm illiterate in 24 languages," he'd brag.

My father's quests for attention could also be three dimensional, particularly after he encountered a course on dying and death. "It happens to one out of one!" he exclaimed. Apparently this was news to him.

When my father was in his 70s, he discovered a college-level pottery class that was free for retirees. Maybe it appealed to him because his father's family had run a pottery in Ukraine, and his father had run a wholesale pottery business in Philadelphia.

Enthusiasm seized my father. He learned to manufacture rectangular objects using slabs of clay and round-sided objects using coils.

He started carrying around a little notepad and sketching things he saw that he thought he could reproduce in clay. It didn't occur to him that most of the time he was stealing ideas that professional artists had created and were selling in stores he'd wandered into.

Once when I was along, he spotted a chimney attached to an abandoned factory. He insisted on postponing whatever I'd planned for us, and sat on a bench to sketch it. When he returned to class, he used five slabs of clay to create a lopsided rectangular vase, a dirty, off-white with black projections, although many feet smaller than the original.

I don't know how many vases and boxes and bowls the other students created during the several courses he ended up taking; my father created lots, foisted them on everyone he knew, and arrived on visits expecting to see them being used. He'd made sure that each recipient couldn't forget who'd made them by creating an artistic signature for himself and etching it into the clay, transforming Ben Shapiro into BENZ. All capital letters that couldn't be missed, with the tail of the Z sometimes trailing off exuberantly beyond the end of the word.

The trouble for me and, I suspected, for the other recipients of his clunky largesse was that his enthusiasm exceeded his talent. By miles. Occasionally my mother would volunteer to incise a decoration into one of his creations, using her genuine artistic talent to improve his work. It was her way of telling him the truth. Me, I didn't have the nerve; instead, I resorted to brooding.

His magnum opus was a trio of individual cylindrical vases, small, medium and large, enlarged copies of cute trios that were being sold in numerous stores. Kids with huge, open mouths and hair he created by squeezing clay through a strainer he'd filched from my mother's kitchen. The biggest kid was nearly two feet tall. And all were excruciatingly ugly. After he glazed them, he brought them home and located them in a very public spot in my mother's otherwise elegant living room. "Why does Grandma let him mess up her house like that?" one of my sons asked after our first post-installation visit. What he was too young to understand, of course, was that "let" was never the right word to describe the way my father operated.

Macramé was another of his very tangible and intrusive hobbies. The same degree of enthusiasm engulfed him and for a while, every time I visited, he'd be sitting with a board on his lap, strings dangling from the board, and sitting to his right, a box of thin, silvery metal push pins that had a habit of escaping and wandering until they settled beneath my mother's vacuum cleaner.

If his designated target was Jewish, he'd be making a wall hanging with a Star of David. If the target was Christian, a hanging featured what he referred to as a Roman Cross.

Hangings weren't the only genre in his canon. He also made mats—mats for bathroom floors, placemats for tables. Sometimes, by folding them or attaching additional knotted strings, he'd morph the mats into other things like clothespin bags and handbags and pillows, almost inevitably in inconvenient sizes.

But, like the pottery, I saw the macramé as merely a means to his traditional end. When the recipient was someone he knew, he'd follow up the gift with a flurry of personal visits, to make sure his hanging was still hanging. If he didn't know a recipient personally, that didn't stop him. The Pope got a cross. Menachem Begin got a star. And there were many other famous recipients.

His ultimate effort: when Prince Charles and Diana got engaged, he sent them a set of four placemats. Not simply through the mail, though. He found someone with an English cousin who happened to be a Member of Parliament. By pulling those metaphorical strings, my father actually got the placemats hand delivered to the side door of Buckingham Palace.

Each of those famous recipients sent a thank-you letter he or she had personally typed or hand written to him. Or so my father believed. He carefully pasted each form letter into a red leatherette-covered scrapbook. Then he carried the scrapbook with him wherever he went. He was particularly fond of going to Elderhostels. His life total: more than 50. My mother was in charge of packing their clothes; about the only thing he managed to pack was his scrapbook.

For many years, my reactions were totally negative, yet even before death stopped my father, three things started me down the road to realizing that I might be mistaken: other photos; an audiologist, and that trio of vases.

The earliest photo arrived two weeks after my younger son's wedding, where my older son's daughter had been given the job of being a flower girl. But for some unstated reason, she refused to wear the garland of fresh flowers that was assigned to her. At the wedding reception, my father made a very public show of grabbing the garland and setting it on his own head, a show at least as embarrassing to me as so many others had been. But the photos included a close-up of my father with the garland on his head. And a smile so big, so happy, so full of life, it forced me to smile too.

Five years later, my father threw himself a ninetieth birthday party. He hired a three-man band and marched, uninvited, with the professional performers around the party room of the retirement community where he and my mother had moved. There are photos of that night as well, photos again showing him so engaged that they eclipse any resentment I feel whenever I come across them and remember his outrageous performance.

It was shortly after the party that my mother fell down and broke a hip, and cascaded over the side of the cliff known as Alzheimer's. My father telephoned and demanded that I travel the thousand miles from Wisconsin to Philadelphia. "She's lost the will to live," he said. His despair was clear. She'd always let him run her life, but the truth as I suddenly saw it was something more: his insistence on her participating in his activities was the rope that had restrained her.

When my mother was moved to the nursing home area of their retirement community, my father was transferred into an assisted living apartment. He was hospitalized at the time, and clearly in need of new hearing aids. Clear to me, anyway, because he had begun to shoehorn his jokes into any given conversation. Because he wanted so desperately to remain a part of a conversation he couldn't hear.

His audiologist had been his doctor for so long that it took no effort on my part to get him to agree to an in-hospital visit. When I went to pick up the results, the new hearing aids, the doctor asked, "What's with Ben? He didn't have a joke to tell me." His despair was as clear in person as my father's had been on the telephone.

Soon my father gave me reason to despair. While he was hospitalized, it fell to me to sort and discard, and move him and whatever remained from his two-bedroom apartment into a one-bedroom unit. Three of the things I didn't discard were those three open-mouthed pottery kids. But he took one look at the trio and demanded, "Why'd you move those things?"

They hadn't gained in attractiveness for me, but I'd moved them because they seemed so emblematic of him. In a good way. After all, he had found that first pottery class because of a long-term habit of searching for courses and Elderhostels that would teach him something new. And his enthusiasm for all his creations, however ill-advised, suddenly seemed the outward evidence of his own will to live. His will to be, and to be remembered.

The farther time moves from the day of my father's death, the more the negative memories recede, and the positives underlying those same events occupy the foreground. When someone else's funeral makes me remember him, I feel the need to eulogize, to praise.

That he left tangible reminders behind no longer bothers me. I cook a meal and put the hot pots on the macramé mats he made for me, and think of him without any trace of bitterness. Never mind that his placemats were always slightly smaller than they should have been to successfully accommodate standard place settings, and were made of string so thick that plates couldn't sit steadily on them. The mats make great landings for casseroles fresh from my oven.

I wash the cooking tools I've used and replace them to the right of my stove, in the five cylinders he stuck together to make a single thick-walled, rust-colored conglomeration with incised black decorations and pathetically thin arms, one of them broken in transit. The design was my mother's idea, though the creation might not have been exactly what she was picturing. No matter— she found the piece hugely practical when it was in her tiny kitchen, and I find it hugely practical in mine.

In valuing the pottery, I am not the only one. As I sought homes for some of the pieces still hanging around, a cousin seized the factory chimney. "It's so him!" Bill exclaimed. It now sits on an end table in his living room.

A few of my memories trigger regret. I think about the way we teased my father when Charles and Diana's divorce was announced, about the way we asked whether he thought the suit would stall over who got the quartet of macramé placemats. I think about his pained reaction, and then it occurs to me that if it weren't for his insatiable curiosity, he wouldn't have found out about the British cousin. Or about so many other things.

I even find myself repeating some of the things that bothered me so much when he did them. After there's a death in the family of a friend, I inevitably find myself working hard to cheer the others who have gathered, though not because I want attention centered on myself.

Is it possible that wasn't his main goal either?

If I hadn't known that this seemingly inappropriate behavior was a religious tradition, I would have discovered it at his graveside funeral, when the rabbi's eulogy included, "And if I say macramé?" This solicited universal belly laughs that carried as far as an automobile where an old friend of my parents waited because her legs and walker couldn't navigate the uneven ground. When the service ended and we returned to the parking lot, the friend demanded, "What was all that laughing about?"

We told her.

She laughed, too.

There are 613 *mitzvot*—commandments or good deeds, depending on how you look at them—and one of them is to bring laughter to a house of mourning.

Maybe I learned that in Hebrew School.

More likely, I learned it by encountering my father.

Like her mother before her and one son after her, **Marilyn Leys** was a teacher for almost all of her working life. She taught high school English and journalism in Milwaukee for 20 years. For 10 of those years, she devised curriculum and taught the Journalism Career Specialty, a magnet program that mashed together print and broadcast newswriting, public relations, and advertising. After she and her husband moved to a farm in southwest Wisconsin, she fell into a job teaching a one-credit journalism course at the University of Wisconsin–Richland.

Some of Leys' freelance articles have found their way into print, but a historical novel involving one wife, two husbands, and the 19th century Wisconsin fur trade is still looking for a publisher.

Melina Claire Hoffman with a few well-trained goats.

THE ART OF WELLNESS

MELINA CLAIRE HOFFMAN

I had just finished milking my neighbor's badly trained goats when Darryl handed me eight pages of music he had written. Those pages finalized my attitude toward him: Darryl was a dream come true. I was sweaty and dirty from having helped my neighbor catch his goats, drag each of them onto the milking stand, and tie their feet so they couldn't kick over the bucket, and then I milked like a maniac. That was my normal morning routine. I was a budding performer, storyteller, and teacher who was drawn to extreme challenges. Darryl was a seasoned composer and author who had been pushing himself to do his creative best for decades. I had asked for his help with a short folk melody two days before. I told him that I wanted to sing it with two other voices and accompany it with my beloved resonator bells, a xylophone-like instrument. He answered my request with a complete choral arrangement.

I looked over the piece in awe and said something like, "How did you do it?" The imagery of his answer has stayed with me ever since: "If my pacing could have dug into the floor, there would be deep ruts in my room by now." He shared his creative process by continuing, "For the past two days, I have been pacing and creating, pacing and creating, pacing and creating. I don't even know how much I have eaten or slept." I admired Darryl immensely. I wanted him to teach me everything he knew.

Like Darryl, I was no stranger to making sacrifices for art. A couple years before I met him, I had given up my life as I knew it. On a day's notice, I left my partner of six years, abandoned my plan to travel in India, and embarked on the path to becoming a performing Eurythmist. Eurythmy is a spiritually based performing art. For me Eurythmy was a flame and I was a moth. I studied Eurythmy, music, storytelling, and spiritual philosophy at a boot-camp-like school. While I was there, I began to live by an artistic ethic that was like a battle cry: Art is the human flame aglow! Burn, burn, burn! Set the Earth aglow!

After a year and a half, I left that Eurythmy school, having gained a mountain of skills and lost an ocean of sleep. I went to live on a farm to re-balance, yet I still yearned for artistic teachers and collaborators who shared my intensity. After a year on the farm, I found a work-exchange position helping to home school an amazing 11-year-old girl on a beautiful, two-acre homestead. Darryl was living down the road from me doing work exchange for rent. I looked up from the goat's udder one spring day and he was walking toward me. I noticed the radiance of his heart region and the childlike innocence of his eyes. Otherwise, he was an unremarkable older man with white hair and glasses. But we found each other quite remarkable.

The first time we met, we talked about my work as a teacher and storyteller. "I am seeking to encourage each child's highest potential and truest intentions," I told him. He nodded intently while I spoke. The next day after I finished milking, he gave me a copy of an article he had written. It stated his life mission: to create art for a purpose beyond his own self-interest. I felt drawn to learn more about him and said, "We need to meet somewhere other than the goat corral." We met at a café in town and had a classic American diner lunch.

I learned that for the past 25 years Darryl had been living in southern California caring for his ailing mother. At 65, he was a recluse whose only devotion was art. His art was entirely driven by his own passion. "The great composers are my friends," he told me. And indeed, he never spoke to me of any living friends. He wrote prolifically, publishing somewhere around 20 books and hundreds of articles. In him, I saw a wellspring of wisdom. In me, he saw a bridge to his newest dream. "After all these years of learning and working alone," he told me, "I am ready to teach." We spoke openly of our meeting as a destiny meeting.

He was the teacher and collaborator I had been looking for. It happened many times that I asked him a question about music and received a brilliant impromptu lecture based on his extensive research. Sitting in my attic studio, I would watch, amazed, as he paced back and forth, his blue eyes flashing, his arms bursting up to the sky to punctuate the importance of Bach's contribution to Western music. He started coming to every storytelling performance I did and writing music for me to play on the bells.

We had known each other for a month when he approached me, folk melody arrangement in hand, after I had finished milking the goats. That was around the time when we both rearranged our lives to maximize our time together. We rescheduled all of our work-exchange hours to the morning, freeing up our afternoons to create. We cut fences free from woody vines and fed the roughage to the goats. We dug shallow trenches for irrigation pipes and hauled the Californian sandy soil away in wheelbarrows. We were always really sweaty and hungry by the time we went back to my attic. He would shower first while I got lunch started, and then I would shower while he finished up the food prep. We chatted amicably, laughed a lot, and enjoyed each other's company over lunch. Then we got down to the real work.

On top of all our other projects, we had one grand performance that we envisioned doing together at some point in the future. He considered his last book to be his masterpiece, the essential and unified expression of his creative impulse. He called it *The Music of the Universe*. The back cover reads: "The universe 'sings.' From the smallest flash of energy to the largest star, everything is a sort of music. That belief lay at the heart of many ancient myths. And now modern science is beginning to discover or rediscover a musical universe." I read the book, loved it, and wanted to bring the soul of it off the page into musical story form. He wanted to write the music for that story. The air around us felt crystalline every time we worked on it; every word we spoke brought the vision to life. *The Music of the Universe* was also the book that got Darryl a teaching position in Boulder, Colorado—a place he had never been before.

Our move from California to Boulder happened because the Eurythmy flame was lit again in my life. I stretched out my moth-wings and flew toward it. In June, on my 30th birthday, I discovered that a new Eurythmy school was starting in Boulder in September. Darryl was happy for me. He could see I was on fire. As a result of my renewed interest in Eurythmy (which had been started by the multitalented philosopher Rudolf Steiner), Darryl started to read Steiner's lectures on music. "I am not alone!" He declared, "Finally, I have found someone else who knows it, too. We are made of music!" I was deeply pleased to witness Darryl's excitement, and I posed him a big question shortly thereafter. "Would you like to move to Boulder with me?" He said he would like nothing more.

I visited Boulder in July to finalize my decision. While meeting with the two founding teachers, I mentioned I would be moving to town with my music theory teacher. One of them exclaimed, "We're looking for a music theory teacher!" I showed them *The Music of the Universe,* and they said he looked like the right man for the job. Darryl and I began preparing for a new life together.

Now, there are a few things I haven't mentioned. Darryl had some odd quirks. At the time, I viewed every single one of them as a surmountable side effect of his genius. I believed in him completely. It turns out, I saw what I wanted to see and disregarded the rest. But once we got to Boulder, the rest became impossible to disregard. He was strangely defensive, to the point of lying, about certain aspects of himself. One day I walked past his room when his door was partly open, and he was angrily berating the wall. "Darryl, are you okay?" I asked. A few moments later he came into the living room and told me, "I can sometimes get very passionate when I practice for classes." I didn't buy his explanation, but didn't let on. I let the incident go. We were artistically thrilled to be in Boulder, and that was all that mattered to me.

The opening ceremony of the Eurythmy school was on his 66th birthday. "This is the best day of my life," he told me. That same day our upstairs neighbor gave him a bike for free. That was exactly what Darryl needed. On that day I had unshakable faith that Darryl and I would live our artistic dreams. Our relationship as roommates quickly came into question.

One day near the end of September, he asked me if he could put pictures of his family on our living room mantel piece. I told him I didn't know his family and would prefer if the living room could be reserved for decoration that had meaning for both of us. He stormed into his room. I went there a few minutes later. He was drinking a cup of water, and he was livid. He threw the water in my face and came at me with his hands poised to choke me. His eyes were jittering back and forth. He looked possessed. I stood there shocked, and, thankfully, he stopped himself. As I turned and walked out of the room, I knew I wasn't safe. Sitting in the living room a few minutes later, I told him, "We can't be roommates anymore. You need to find a new place to live." He was distraught. "Who am I?" he said. "You're the person I love most in the world, and I attacked you. I'm not qualified to be a teacher." I tried to reassure him. "People lose their tempers sometimes, and it doesn't mean they can't be good teachers." We both agreed it would be best if he moved out.

A few days later Darryl was to teach his first class. That morning I wished him a good day, had a fine day at school myself, and then rode the bus home. I had a very striking musical experience on that bus ride. I had been trying for the past week to remember the tune to an Irish folk song called "Danny Boy." I knew I had heard the tune, but I just couldn't fully remember it. As I sat on the bus yearning to catch a strand of it, I suddenly heard it being sung in the distance somewhere above me. I froze and listened with my inner ear. A choir of gorgeous voices was singing every note of it:

> Oh Danny Boy, the pipes, the pipes are calling.
> From glen to glen and down the mountainside.
> The Summer's gone and all the flowers are dying.
> 'Tis you, 'tis you must go and I must bide.
> But come ye back when Summer's in the meadow
> Or when the valley's hushed and white with snow.
> 'Tis I'll be here in sunshine or in shadow
> Oh Danny Boy I love you so.

I floated home on clouds of awe and gratitude blissfully singing "Oh Danny Boy." I arrived home, took the garage-door clicker out of my bag, and pressed the grey button. The garage door rumbled up. I stared death in the face. Darryl was hanging dead from a rope in the garage.

I ran past him and called 911. Thank goodness for the dispatcher. She waited on the line while I went outside and screamed, "No, No, No!" again and again. Thank goodness for all the help that arrived shortly thereafter. Firefighters, police, paramedics, coroners, and victims' advocates were all there within minutes. One of my Eurythmy teachers came that evening, and my entire new community surrounded me with massive quantities of support in the months that followed.

But nothing was able to shield me from being totally blindsided by grief. I had no concept that grief could make a person physically and psychologically ill. It turns out it can. I had no appetite. I felt like I was in a fog. I pushed a cart aimlessly around the grocery store thinking, "I must eat to live. I am not allowed to leave this store until I put something in this cart." I was constantly exhausted during the day but couldn't sleep at night. Many times I walked into the apartment, where Darryl no longer lived, and just passed out on the floor. My heart raced like a frightened mouse, and I sometimes wondered why it even bothered to beat at all. After many months of deep grief, I was able to think again. I had to rethink my life.

The death of my beloved teacher and friend shattered the intensity of living for art alone. I saw clearly that prolific creation did not make him well. My will to be well became my new priority. I fantasized that if I met another genius, I would say, "I'm so glad you're such a genius! Let's do lunch. Let's be on fire together for a few hours. Then you can go home to feast on your ecstasy and agony till you collapse; I'll go home, make a healthy dinner, and go to bed shortly thereafter."

And now, I often do just that: I will interrupt my music making to brush my teeth and go to bed. I am creating a new, healthy artistic ethic. Joy and ripeness are my new teachers. I sing in a trio with two friends, and we have a fantastic time. We sing the songs that bring us joy and perform them when they are ripe. I play resonator bells when I am moved to, and their ringing is deeply nourishing for me every time.

In the beauty and warmth of the Waldorf Kindergarten where I now teach, storytelling and music are woven into my daily life. The school is also a mini-farm, with gardens and chickens and a herd of docile goats. So docile that they can be still while a group of three-year olds pet them. I am not as artistically prolific as I could be if I slept less or pushed myself more. But this spring I will have the delightful opportunity of milking some really well-trained goats.

MELINA CLAIRE HOFFMAN is a storyteller and creative educator in Boulder, Colorado. She specializes in co-creating kindness and joy through story and song with children at Boulder Waldorf Kindergarten, Nevei Kodesh (a Jewish Renewal Congregation), and private family homes. Her storytelling ranges from folklore and participatory improv for kids to mystical teaching tales for adults.

"The burning image I hold of Jack is of him standing on the front porch of his home in upstate New York, waving me off as I drove away, never to see him again."

Nurse Log:
A Radical Departure

Jerry Wennstrom

An enormous slab of cedar was sitting on the beach where I live. The sand and tide had worn the shape of the wood, revealing an image of a woman with her right arm held high above her head. I brought the cedar home and left it leaning up against my barn, where it stayed for the next year. Over the course of that year, I occasionally glanced at the slab, pondering what I might do with it. I finally brought it into my studio after returning from a trip to New York where I had spent a couple of weeks with my younger brother who was dying of cancer.

Knowing when I left him that we would probably never see each other again, I found myself haunted by images of limitation and death. I had witnessed the shadow of limitation as it moved progressively over his life, burning its bridges as it went, leaving no way back to more of anything.

One day when I was visiting with Jack, and even though he was very weak, with a show of bravado he decided to go outside and help his pleading young son, Jared, get his all-terrain vehicle started. Seconds into the attempt he stopped dead in his tracks, as if he had been hit between the eyes with a 2" x 4" and retreated back to his not-so-easy chair.

During one of my feeble attempts at inspiring conversation, he tried to remain present and awake, only to apologize while dropping off to sleep. Saddest of all was a moment when Joann, my sister-in-law, offered me some potato chips. I took one and ate it and when offered another said, "No thanks, I don't really like unsalted potato chips." Hearing me, Jack looked wistfully over at the bag of chips and said, "I love potato chips." Knowing he couldn't eat, I held back tears . . . my heart breaking.

After spending those two weeks in close proximity to death, on my return home I saw death everywhere. Yet contrary to the constant companionship of death, an answer to my prayers arrived miraculously at an unexpected moment. It happened on the phone, and it snapped me into a kind of unconditional attention at a moment when my brother needed me the most. The encounter overrode all limitations and flung open the gates to the inevitability of death.

The burning image I hold of Jack is of him standing on the front porch of his home in upstate New York, waving me off as I drove away, never to see him again.

Moments before I was sitting in the living room with him, Joann, and Jared. Jared was crashing cars on a video game he was playing on their wide screen TV while Joann commented on his bad "driving." Knowing I had to leave in a few minutes to catch my flight home, I was tempted to ask if they would turn off the TV so we could have some quiet time together.

After sitting for a few moments, trying to decide what to do, I realized that Jack was dying, everyone was sad, and the TV might just be what everyone needed. Once I had resigned myself to the situation, the TV went off, Jared went outside to play, and Joann got up and went into the kitchen. Miraculously, Jack and I were left alone to say our good-byes. After a few minutes, sitting quietly together, I turned to Jack and said, "I have to leave soon, you know." We silently looked at each other for a long sad moment. Then Jack said, "Will we see each other again?" We both knew in that instant that we wouldn't, so we just held one another and cried.

Eventually, after our awkward and teary good-byes, I made my way out to the car. I was feeling so very sad but knowing I needed to compose myself for the two-hour drive to the airport. Sitting quietly in the car for a few emotional moments with my eyes closed, I said a little prayer for Jack. On opening my eyes, I was startled to see him standing on the porch looking at me with such love in his eyes. I waved, took a picture, and drove away in a fog of sad/happy/loving feelings for him—thankful for the gift we received in the raw vulnerability of our last moments on Earth together.

After returning home, I occasionally called Jack and spoke with him for as long as he was able. Aware of his limited energy and sensitive to any sign of fatigue, I tried to keep our conversations real and efficient. During what was to be our very last conversation, I sensed he was on an edge, struggling physically, mentally, and emotionally.

Feeling my deep love for him in that instant, I gave myself completely to death itself, letting it take me wherever it needed to go! Shooting from the hip, I said, "Jack, dying is what you are doing now, and there is nothing else to do." With unstoppable determination, I spoke passionately about the inherent loneliness of life and how there was no avoiding death for any of us. I told him how brave and uncomplaining he had been throughout his entire illness and how proud I was of him. I told him that he was showing us how it might be done with dignity and grace.

Relieved at having the difficult loneliness of his suffering acknowledged, his response was selfless and emotional. He simply said, "I didn't want my family to suffer." We were both overcome with emotion, and there was nothing more to say. My older brother John, who was with him at the time, then took the phone and told me that Jack was crying uncontrollably. So was I.

Having the slab of cedar in my studio and continuing to be haunted by death, I began carving the lower part, which became a woman's body, in skeletal form. Making my way upward, the image transitioned into embodied flesh. Life was growing out of death. To further enhance the theme, I placed the carved figure inside of a hollowed-out, decaying log and called the piece "Nurse Log." A nurse log in the wild is a dead tree that has become host to new life. The new life often takes the form of a seedling tree that grows off of its host and feeds on the nutrients released by its natural decay.

Perhaps I was trying to rise up and out of the gravity of my recent experience of the death of my brother. For the most part, the image at that stage was hopeful and positive. It was a skeleton becoming flesh and reaching upward out of death and decay. Her eyes were open and her face was transcendent and bright. But I was struggling with the hopefulness of this piece, never quite feeling that what was being expressed was quite "IT."

My wife loved it and saw in the image hope and a new direction for our lives. My friend and benefactor came to see the new art piece and liked it also, seeing a new and hopeful direction. He felt I was expressing a larger collective hopefulness and new beginning.

Unfortunately, even with the generous praise I was receiving, I could not shake the feeling that the piece had not broken through to that place of inspiration. I had nothing against hope, yet there was something that left me feeling flat. At a deeper level, I sensed the "Nurse Log" did not embrace the deeper mystery and paradox of death and renewal.

Joseph Campbell said, (to paraphrase) art that has "an agenda," even if that agenda is positive, can only be "propaganda." He went on to say that inspired creation simply leaves one in a state awe.

Feeling less than awed, I simply sat with the art piece for several days. At one point, I placed a hammered, brass platter behind the head of the figure and installed a light, which illuminated the indentations at the edges, giving it the appearance of a halo. This move somehow rang true, enhancing the spiritual quality of the figure I was trying to achieve. Meditating on the image further, I felt it had taken on the look of a Russian icon, and the deeper mystery of the Christian mythos began to stir into the mix.

I then carved a second, iconic, face and placed it over the first. I cut the mask-like overlay roughly in half and hinged it so it opened at the center to reveal the now-hidden inner face. Having done this, I felt the piece had at least begun its approach into deeper paradox.

Happy with the further developments but still not inspired, I did something that felt like an outrageous act of faith. I hammered a 12-inch forged steel nail through the upraised hand and painted blood oozing from the wound. I knew the piece was complete.

Hammering the nail through the hand was a difficult inspiration to act on. I had hesitated for a moment, then immediately chose to take action and not to give it any more thought. In retrospect, I believe it was a way for me to jump back into the *Now*, and in doing so, relinquish all controls and contrived possible outcomes. I was abandoning the idea of "hope," false or otherwise, and handing life and death back to the gods for them to do with it what they will. It was a way of saying, "Yes, there is life and there is death and I am here for all of it!"

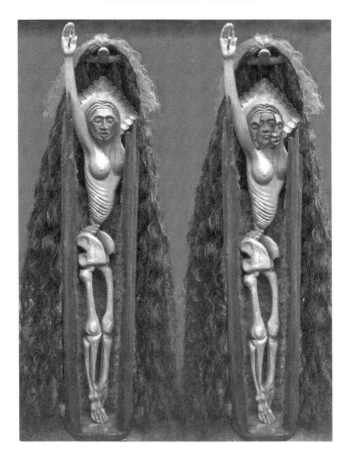

JERRY WENNSTROM is an artist, author of *The Inspired Heart: An Artist's Journey of Transformation* (book and audiobook) and subject of Parabola and Sentient Publications documentary videos, *In the Hands of Alchemy* and *Studio Dialogue*. Jerry's art is featured in the film *Mythic Journeys*. His unusual life story is currently being made into a feature film by award-winning Danish filmmaker Hans Fabian Wullenweber. Jerry has traveled with his wife Marilyn Strong internationally, lecturing, teaching, showing the films and presenting their work. Together they created the six-month program Thresholds: Exploring Passageways to the Soul through Dreamwork, Ritual and the Creative Process.

(from left) Carolyn, Susan, and Judy in October 2002. Judy died in March 2004.

*"Judy was respected as a wise counselor, a trusted friend,
a sponsor to others new in recovery, an inspiration to many."*

A Sister's Lasting Imprint

BY CAROLYN KOTT WASHBURNE

S usan and I are about to get our sister Judy's ashes into the ground, a mere eight years after her death. This foot dragging is partly because of initial snafus by the cemetery—first they ordered the wrong granite, and then they placed Judy's headstone off center and upside down—and partly because we have been reluctant to say our final good-byes.

Judy certainly would have made a wisecrack about the delay, something like: "What's the rush, you slackers? I'll be dead for forever."

You didn't want to be on the receiving end of Judy's wit. A teacher in the Chicago Public Schools, she had a 16-year-old (only a sixth grader, by the way) who didn't like that she threatened to fail him. He said, "Miss Kott, if I don't pass this test, I'm gonna have my boys come and visit you." To which Judy replied, "If they're as stupid as you are, they won't even be able to find the school."

She made up memorable words and phrases. A "spider-faced bitch" was any female she didn't like. Her school administrators were "incompetent bunglers." "Stickler Bob" was a neighbor she found too fussy.

Although three years younger than I, Judy could be a formidable adversary. In 1957, she "borrowed" (without permission) my crinoline. When I retaliated by "borrowing" one of her slips, Judy launched a stealth counterattack that left my closet and chest of drawers almost empty. I dreaded coming home from school to discover what else might be gone.

Yet her generosity was legendary. As a young person, she insisted on bringing home every broken-winged bird and half-dead mouse for rehabilitation. As a teacher, she inspired some of Chicago's toughest students, including those born to crack-addicted mothers she'd had in class 20 years earlier. Going through her papers after her death, we discovered an organized and detailed checklist of Christmas gifts she had bought for disadvantaged children. The chart listed age, gender, type of gift, and possibilities for the following year.

Intensely intelligent, she could beat the pants off of everyone at Trivial Pursuit and Jeopardy! She loved brain teasers.

Legendary in a not-good way were Judy's struggles with alcohol and drugs. She began drinking beer in high school, sneaking out of her first-floor bedroom window to meet like-minded friends. One night she came home drunk and drove the family car into a tree.

In college at the University of Colorado at Boulder (a perfect fit for a party girl), she got expelled from her sorority. No surprise: substance abuse was involved. In the mid-'60s on a family trip to New York City, Judy went out one night and didn't return. The next morning our frantic parents were about to notify the police when she walked in the door, slightly disheveled but smiling. "How is everybody?"

Being an adult in the workforce didn't stop the substance abuse. She bragged about having a bottle of vodka in her desk drawer at school to "get through the day." On a Caribbean cruise with our mother and aunt, she was so wired that three days into the cruise, the crew put her off the ship. She had been running up and down the decks, hallucinating and talking incoherently.

Our family tried to intervene: "Judy, we love you and we think you are sick and need help. We'll stick by you, but we don't want to be with you or talk to you on the phone when you're loaded." Susan refused to let Judy attend her wedding unless she came sober, which Judy did, but left early. Judy tried inpatient rehab two or three times; it didn't take. "It's easier to get drugs in rehab than it is on the street," she reported.

Then, in 1987, she almost died from an overdose of cocaine and alcohol. Everyone was surprised that she lived. She was medically managed through detox. She hobbled her way to AA. She got clean and sober and stayed clean and sober. She divorced her drug-dealer husband. She began taking medication for bipolar disorder, undiagnosed for all those years. She became a fixture at her AA club.

Being with a sober Judy was like seeing a life reborn. She enjoyed 17 years of real living. Of living life as it always should have been. Of hugging her nieces and nephews, bringing thoughtful gifts, laughing and joking. I once saw my mother smiling while looking at Judy, at peace with a daughter who was once lost.

Then Judy's body began to fail. We knew *something* was wrong—Judy weighed less than 90 pounds (she was about 5 feet 7), slept 12 hours a day, and had trouble getting out of a chair. When we urged her to get help, she told us she was "handling it." One doctor thought it was acid reflux and gave her medication. Finally Judy, a smoker since high school, visited an oncologist on a Thursday, where she received the diagnosis of Stage 4 lung cancer (there is no Stage 5). The doctor then said, "Of course, you'll quit smoking," to which Judy replied, "Hell, no!" If she had lived, it's unlikely that she would have had chemo or radiation. Judy always did things in her own way and on her own timetable.

Judy died the following Wednesday. The doctors had put in a breathing tube to keep her alive until I could drive two hours to get there. Before she was intubated, Susan put a phone to Judy's ear so we could say a few final words.

"Grrrak muffjl purccch," came through my cell phone.

"I love you, Judy," I replied, "and I forgive you for taking my crinoline in 1957." I meant it to be funny. I think I heard a garbled laugh from her.

When I arrived, she was unconscious, but I like to think she heard the loving words I whispered in her ear. After the doctor removed the tube, five of us—Susan and I, Judy's boyfriend, Susan's husband, and a family friend—gathered around the bed. Judy loved the Serenity Prayer ("God, grant me the serenity to accept the things I cannot change . . . "), so we said it as group as we held her hands. She died shortly after. She was 57.

As Susan and I talked with people at Judy's visitation and funeral, we were shocked to learn about a very different sister than the one we thought we knew. With family, she was often brusque and caustic, never wanting to talk about feelings, typically wisecracking even in serious moments. With her AA community, Judy was respected as a wise counselor, a trusted friend, a sponsor to others new in recovery, an inspiration to many. One person after another told us how much of an impact she'd had:

"Judy saved my marriage and my job."

"Judy got me back on track when I developed a gambling addiction. She lent me money to pay off my debts and then *made me* stick to the repayment schedule."

"Judy literally saved my life—if she hadn't confronted me on my denial and bullshit, I'd be dead today."

"She left a lasting imprint on our hearts."

Learning about Judy's generosity has made me want to give of my time and emotional resources as she did. I now volunteer as a cook at a meal program. I read to a blind friend every week. As a freelance writer, I take on pro bono projects for nonprofits. I ghostwrote a memoir for a friend about her years with an abusive husband. With my college writing students, I try to be patient and supportive yet candid about what they need to improve on.

Most important, I work to be more accepting of others' shortcomings (I have none, of course!) and yet be more honest. Judy and I had a difficult relationship, because of birth order issues and because of differences in our personalities and styles. After her death, I regretted the things I said that I shouldn't have and the things I should have said but didn't. I've learned not to let the sun go down on an argument or difficult situation.

And so, in a few weeks when we lay Judy to rest—hopefully with her headstone right side up and centered below our parents' stones—I'll give thanks for her life and for the inspiration she bequeathed us.

KOTT WASHBURNE has been a freelance writer and editor for over 35 years. She is the author of seven nonfiction books, and her articles have appeared in *The New York Times, International Herald Tribune, Utne Reader, Mademoiselle, Ms.* and *Milwaukee Magazine.* She is also an Adjunct Associate Professor Emerita in the Department of English at the University of Wisconsin-Milwaukee.

Nataliya Bukhanova, Dmitrij Bukhanov (1978-2004),
Valentin Alexandrovich Bukhanov (1948-1995).

*"I still keep an old photo: my Dad, my brother, and me on
the top of a hill. Looking at it, I realize that I am the only
one of the three of us who is alive now."*

DEATH DOES NOT
HAVE A FACE

NATALIYA BUKHANOVA

D eath does not have a face, but people do.

When I remember the people who died, I see their faces, and hear their voices in my mind. I recollect their memories, which are alive in me, their reflections, and their thoughts. It is very strange, this collection of memories of the dead people, their last thing that is left here, on the Earth. These memories make them live and speak, feel and move. Sometimes I recollect these pieces of life that is no more and think: did it really exist? Where will it all go when I die and nobody remembers it?

My father said one time, "If only I could start my life again!" He was already terribly sick that year: he had cancer. Hearing those words, I was surprised. My father was a university professor, a brilliant scientist, recognized in our country and abroad, a happy husband, and the head of our family. Very often he spoke to me as to an adult, telling me about science, about history that he was teaching, and about the problems of modern world.

I absorbed every his word like a sponge, but I knew that I could not remember everything that he was saying. Those years, in my early teens, this terrible thought found me: if I would not remember his talks, they would disappear. One time I took a pen and a paper to write down all that my father would say. Having known my intentions, he laughed and took a paper from me. "It is not necessary," he said smiling. For me it was necessary and important, his every word, every little thought. I tried to imagine everything that my Dad was telling, and I knew that one day it would be not his memories, but mine, and they would be very different from his. I was sorry about his world slipping away, about everything that he did not have time to say to me. He said, "If I could start my life again, I would do things differently." Then he said, "I did everything that I had wanted to do in my life." Soon after that he died.

I often ask myself whether I would do anything differently in my life. Usually the answer is "No." Most things happen in their time and their place. Except death.

My younger brother inherited our dad's sense of humour and optimism. My brother was gentle, hard working, and ambitious. One time he said, "I will work until I am 40, then I want to retire and enjoy life." He did not have time to enjoy life: he died in a car crash when he was 26. He had postponed his life for later, working and building a future that never came. After his death I took a notebook and wrote down everything that I remembered about him. I filled hundreds of pages with small events of everyday life, of our childhood and teen ages, with everything that we had in common and everything about us that was different.

I still keep that notebook, although I will never read it again. Now I understand: our memories are so precious, but often we pass by them without a second thought. Now I know why people write memoirs. They want to save and keep the lives of the people dear to them, even when they die, to save impressions about places that changed forever, to return to times that are no more.

It is very simple not to postpone life for the future, to live and enjoy life every moment, at every place, here and now. And you know what? I understood that deep grief is a part of life. Taking pills against the grief was not right, I should have to live through it, only then I was able to understand life as a whole. People without feelings are like machines, and no more. I did not hide myself from sadness. It was hard, though. Hard to live each day, hard to write that book about my brother, a book that is not interesting to anybody except me. One dark evening sitting at my computer, I wrote to one forum (I do not remember which one): "My brother is dead, what to do?" It was an impulsive action; I did not understand why I had done this, and I did not expect anything in response. A lot of people answered me. I received dozens of emails every day, with the words of sympathy, compassion and warmth. I did not feel any better, but I discovered that there were many people ready to help me, whom they did not know, and who felt sorrow for my brother who had been unknown to them. I discovered that I was not alone. I still embrace each moment of my life, I let myself feel everything: joy, gladness, excitement, and grief. I also try to help people. Sometimes a couple of words or even a hug can do better than psychotherapy.

Sometimes I wonder what my child would say. In fact, he could not say anything, because he could not speak. I do not even know if it was a boy or a girl. My child died 10 weeks after he had been conceived. Death took him before he could enter this world, before he could experience anything in life. The doctors said such things could happen and it was not my fault. They said, "You will have other children." But this one will never live again.

When I see children playing I think, they are so lucky to live! We all are so lucky! We can feel, we can think, we can love each other. We often take such things as granted, but in fact, all of this is a blessing.

I still keep an old photo: my Dad, my brother, and me on the top of a hill. Looking at it, I realize that I am the only one of the three of us who is alive now. Death is reality; it is a part of life. I can be afraid of it, I can respect it or pretend that I do not notice it, but it exists anyway. What I think about it is my own choice. I do not close my eyes on death, and I live.

Death does not have a face, but I have written not about death. I have written about love. Life is precious, as well as time with loved ones is. Tell the people who are dear to you about your love; respect and remember your dead ones. It is so simple and so important.

NATALIYA BUKHANOVA was born in Russia. She is a writer, visual artist, and scientist who came to Canada in 2007. Since then her stories have been published in Russian community newspapers in North America, in *Alternative Trends, The Flavours of Edmonton*, the anthologies *Arena-3* and *The World on a Maple Leaf*, and *Writing on the Margins*, as well as in online magazines. She mostly writes short fiction, fantasy, horror, and nonfiction. Recently she published her book of short stories *The Stories by Meranza* (in Russian). Blog: www.meranza.blogspot.com

Honor Quain rests with her father James Quain
a few hours before his death.

*"My own big, disorderly family had gathered to be near him,
and he stayed with us for two days as we laughed and cried
and sang him into the next world."*

TALE OF TWO FUNERALS

PEGINE QUAIN

It seems like a lifetime ago that my mentor called to see if I might be interested in talking to a family in Belmont about a home funeral. Belmont is about 25 miles south of my home in San Francisco; I have friends who live there and I am somewhat familiar with the area, so I agreed to contact the family and called them later that day. On Monday, I packed up my home funeral kit and a suitcase complete with funeral clothes, not knowing how long I would be there or how involved they would want me to be. My friends were leaving the country and were happy to have me stay at their house.

Throughout the consultation and subsequent interactions with the family, I was reminded again and again of my own family. There were so many similarities: a big family with devout Catholic parents, self-directed children, deceased siblings, blue collar work ethics, and disparate personalities all united in their devotion to and obvious love for their father and husband, the man who lay dying, Gino. After I met with them, they decided that yes, in fact, they would like my assistance. I would direct them through the cleansing, dressing, and preserving of their father's body, and the mortuary would take care of the transportation and the paperwork. They had already purchased a beautiful casket handmade by Trappist Monks.

I really liked them and I could tell that they liked me. I told them at the beginning that although I was trained as a home funeral guide, I had never actually assisted with a home funeral on my own, and they had taken it in stride. They were ready to sign the contract, but I didn't even have a business card much less a contract, so we left it at a handshake. I looked back at the house as I was leaving—Gino and his brother had built it themselves back in the '50s. It seemed appropriate that he was going to pass his final days there. Now the only thing left to do was wait, so I walked back to my friends' house. They lived that close.

On Tuesday, I waited and read and reread the funeral guide handbook. On Wednesday, I waited and checked and rechecked my home funeral kit. On Thursday, I decided to call to make sure they hadn't lost my number. They assured me that they hadn't. That was about 10:00 a.m. At 11:30 they called me back to say they were ready. When I arrived, there were people everywhere, washing windows and cooking and busy, I suspect just for the sake of something to do. I went into Gino's room with his wife and one of his daughters and started preparing the space for washing the body. After a while we were joined by one of the sons.

We all worked together in a rhythm that suggested we had done this before. His hair was washed and combed, his body lovingly bathed, his clothes picked out. When we were finished, Gino was resplendent in his favorite square dance clothes with a bolo tie around his neck and a rosary in his hands. His brother Mario sat by his side. Birds of paradise and roses from my friends' garden adorned the bedside table, and a little altar was set up on the other side of the room. His eyes closed in the sleep of Morpheus, he looked serene. It was close to the weekend and Palm Sunday, the beginning of Holy Week and a very busy time in the Catholic Church, so they decided that he would not be buried until Monday. We agreed that I would come back every day until then to check on them and change the dry ice used to preserve the body. It was 3:00 p.m. I returned to my friends' house and read the handbook again, sure that I had missed something. It had gone seamlessly.

An hour later I received a call from my sister in St. Louis saying that our father had had a massive cerebral hemorrhage and that I should make plans to come home. How strange it was that while I was washing and caring for Gino, leading a brother and sister and their mother through the ritual cleansing and dressing of their father and husband, that my own father was dying. I got little sleep that night. I went back to Gino's one more time late the next morning, showing the brothers how to replenish the dry ice and explaining about my own father's condition. I left them confident and comfortable with the task and gave them back-up numbers to call if they had any questions or began to doubt their own abilities. They were grateful. Gino's wife offered her condolences to me as I was leaving. No one could have predicted this turn of events.

I made arrangements to fly out that night. I would leave straight from Belmont, my suitcase still packed with the funeral clothes I had brought with me. I walked down to the bus stop where I had dropped my friends a few days before and caught the express bus bound for the airport. I wouldn't arrive in St. Louis until dawn on Saturday. Sitting on the plane, I thought back on the times that my parents had visited and how much they had enjoyed walking around the neighborhood. They would attend Sunday mass at St. Phillips and then wander down the street to get fresh bagels, marveling at the Victorian houses in the neighborhood, so different from the brick-and-stone architecture of St. Louis. My father liked the Irish priest at St. Phillips, and often times they would go to mass again during the week when it would be said to a smaller gathering in the chapel. He made friends with one of the older parishioners, an elderly woman who lived alone on Alvarado Street, and had me bring her flowers one year just because. That's the kind of guy he was.

My sister met me at the airport just as the sun was coming up, and we drove straight to the hospital. My father, still in intensive care, would come home the next morning. I stayed with him in his room Sunday night, conscious of the changing patterns of his breathing. I spent most of the night talking to him and holding his hand. It was easy to be there but almost unbearable knowing that I would have to let him go.

My own big, disorderly family had gathered to be near him, and he stayed with us for two days as we laughed and cried and sang him into the next world. There were 12 of us around his bed when he died just after 1:00 a.m. on Tuesday morning. As people said their final goodbyes and wandered off in search of a bed or a drink, my mother and sister and I waited for hospice to find their way to the house and make the pronouncement. It was after 3:00 a.m. when they finally left and my mother, exhausted, fell into bed while two of my sisters and one of my brothers and I began the sacred work of bathing and anointing our beloved Pop.

Washing his hair, I couldn't help but think of Gino. It was as if he were there with us. We took our time, being ever so gentle as we worked our way down to his toes. We dressed him according to our mother's wishes, and when we were done, he looked handsome, so Irish in his hand-knit sweater from Donegal, his beads in hand, and his shoes polished to a high shine the way he always wore them. I think he would've been pleased. The candle that had been burning since we brought him home went out and a new one was lit. The room felt like a sanctuary with the morning light, just beginning to break, shining through the

Celtic cross that hung in the window. The dogwood blossoms freshly cut from trees in the yard were luminous at his bedside. It was 5:00 a.m., Tuesday of Holy Week. I'd had nine hours of sleep since I left Belmont.

Later that day my nephew would begin building the plain pine box that would become my father's coffin, brothers and cousins joining in as the day went on. At my mother's request, we all painted our hands and left our prints and messages to Pop on the lid. That night there was an incredible thunder-and-lightning display of the kind you only see in the Midwest, and it ripped open the heavens. It was so powerfully beautiful and so fitting. We held a wake at the house the next day and had glorious weather. People came and went bringing food, telling stories, and paying their respects. Children ran in and out of Pop's room, taping pictures to the wall and telling stories of their own.

We brought the coffin into the kitchen the next morning and laid it on the floor. Grandsons and great grandsons, sons and sons-in-law all helped to move the body and place him gently into the casket. White roses and pictures, notes and charms, a baseball and candy from the little ones all went into the casket with him before it was sealed. He was carried to a friend's van and driven to the church, where friends and parishioners gathered for a final goodbye. We laid out colored markers, and as people came up to offer their condolences, they also wrote their own thoughts and messages on the casket. Children drew flowers.

The service began with my dear friend singing "Smile" a cappella and then, with his four-year-old daughter by his side, my brother read the poem "Thanks" by W. S. Merwin. A poignant eulogy was delivered by my brother-in-law and then the homily by the parish priest before we processed to the veterans' cemetery, where my father received military honors including a 21-gun salute for time spent on Iwo Jima and in Korea. It was Holy Thursday.

The funeral committee, made up of parishioners, had prepared a luncheon for any and all who wished to return to the church cafeteria. Such was their generosity. The place was packed. After everyone was served, my mother rose to address us. She introduced her children one by one and spoke with pride and gratitude for the contributions each had made in caring for our father. She then spoke to her other family, her fellow parishioners, and warmly thanked them for everything they had done to aid and assist us, not only during the last week but over the last 40 years. They are some of her oldest friends. We returned to my parents' house afterword, and a while later everyone left for their own homes, exhausted with grief. I would file the death certificate myself a few days later.

Gino's daughter called me while I was still in St. Louis to express her gratitude and to let me know that Gino's funeral had gone off without any problems. She said that her family thought of me often, knowing that we were sharing a very similar grief. Gino's wife sent me a thank-you card a few weeks later and said that by having Gino at home, each family member was able to envelop him in love in their own time and way and hold him in tender respect through his final passage.

My father and Gino will be forever linked in my memory, beautiful men both in life and in death. Their funerals were held during the holiest week of the year for Catholics, and even though I am no longer an active member of that faith, I felt that it was indeed a sacred time for me, too. I am so thankful to my mentor for giving me the tools and the confidence to go forward when I was in doubt and for giving me the opportunity to test myself and explore the passion that brought me into this work. Guided by something unseen and buoyed by the prayers and thoughts that had been gathered in my name, I had done my first two home funerals in the span of one week. I couldn't imagine a better beginning.

I now have a name for my fledgling business; I call it Family Rites. And even though I am still a novice, I know that I am on the right path and that my father is still with me, showing me the way. Thanks, Pop.

PEGINE QUAIN is a member of the National Home Funeral Alliance and the Funeral Consumers Alliance. She received a certificate of completion in home funeral studies in 2010 from Final Passages in Sebastapol, California and continues her education through workshops and seminars. She is the founder of Family Rites, a business dedicated to the education and empowerment of families interested in caring for their loved ones after death. To find out more about home funerals visit *www.familyrites.com* or write to pegine@familyrites.com

Arrow's body is carried by his friends to the family car
in a hand decorated cardboard casket.

"Our community had had a real initiation in supporting a family choosing to provide after-death care for their beloved at home. For four years the Threshold Care Circle had quietly and steadily held this possibility as an option, and now there were enough people who knew what to do that a whole network sprang into being in a few hours."

THE CALL

CHARLENE ELDERKIN

On a Sunday afternoon in early June, I headed to the Chula Vista Resort in the Wisconsin Dells to give a presentation on home funerals. I had been invited to speak to the Wisconsin Coroners and Medical Examiners conference by the Columbia County Coroner, who had located me through the organization I founded in 2006, the Threshold Care Circle. TCC serves as a community resource for southwestern Wisconsin to educate and empower families who wish to care for their own at the time of death. Although it is perfectly legal to care for a deceased family member at home in Wisconsin, it is not well known, even among coroners. I hoped to shed some light on the subject.

I had been working on my ninety-minute presentation for weeks. The PowerPoint I'd prepared articulated what a home funeral is, why families make that choice, the benefit of doing so, and how coroners and MEs could be of service to home funeral families. It included photos from home funerals that the Threshold Care Circle was connected to. I kept rearranging the slides to find just the right flow.

Four weeks before the conference, our community in Viroqua, Wisconsin, had suffered a terrible loss. At 2 a.m. on Mothers Day my co-worker, Arwyn Wildingway, got the knock on the door that we all hope never to answer. A group of teenagers driving on a country road after prom went off the road, and the two teenaged boys sitting on the passenger side were killed when the side of the car hit a tree. Arrow Wildhack, Arwyn's firstborn, eighteen-year-old son, died, along with his seventeen-year-old friend Nate. The two girls in the car survived.

As Arwyn sat in shock next to her deceased son at the hospital, Janet Reed, the Vernon County Coroner, asked her which funeral home to call. Arwyn answered, "I want to wash him at home." Janet, who was no stranger to families caring for their own at home, understood.

Susan Nesbit, one of our five TCC consultants, was one of the first to know about Arrow's death. Arrow's stepfather, Frank, had called Susan in the early hours of the morning trying to get a message through to one of Arrow's siblings who was staying at a friend's. The phone number he had been calling was not being answered; maybe Susan would know who else to call. "He should hear the news from me," Frank said.

As the sun rose and word spread like a dense fog settling over the community, grieving teenagers, neighbors, and friends instinctively began gathering at the Wildingway home. No one was turned away, and there was no holding back. The grief shared by every parent, every teen, every child was too new, too terrible to be denied. Arwyn was literally held up by a woman on either side of her for the next two days. Later that morning when Susan called to offer assistance, Arwyn affirmed that she wanted to bring Arrow home.

There were so many grief-stricken people gathered at the house, and so many things that needed doing. Susan arrived at the Wildingway home and started delegating. She made cleaning assignments. She gave a trusted family friend the task of gathering all the required paperwork and seeing that it was filled out properly. The open front porch was designated as the place Arrow would lie in honor, so fabric needed to be draped to give the space privacy.

Susan located a handmade wooden casket for Arrow to be placed in during the home visitation time. Another TCC member delivered a cardboard cremation coffin, setting it up outside on a stand, along with art supplies to encourage mourners to artfully adorn the coffin. She also brought our "death midwifery kit" containing the supplies needed to care for the body, along with a massage table upon which Arrow would be washed and dressed.

Around 3 p.m. it was time to pick up Arrow's body from the hospital morgue. Susan drove her van as the transporting vehicle, and Arwyn rode behind in another car with a small group of friends. Arrow's body was in the body bag required for transport. It would be a relief to get him home and release him from the bag. A circle of friends assembled at the house to care for the body, not really knowing what to expect. Arrow had donated eyes, heart valves, bones, and tissue. All willingly stretched beyond their comfort zones to support their grieving friend. Arwyn washed the face of her son; the circle of women cared for the rest of his body with tears, prayers, and gentle caresses, washing, dressing and placing him in the wooden casket on the porch.

Although dry ice is often used for cooling the body, in our rural area it is not very accessible, so we utilize a reusable product called Techni ice™. The ice that had been divided up among TCC members was now gathered and delivered for use. Susan assigned two women to "ice duty"—changing the ice every eight hours to ensure that the body was kept cool. Vigil assignments were given so that Arrow would always have someone with him, but Arwyn chose to spend that first night alone with her son on the cold porch.

It was a windy and cool Monday morning when I arrived at the family home to pay my respects. The sidewalk was already filled with chalk drawings of hearts and arrows. The cardboard coffin set up in the driveway was being decorated with drawings and farewell messages.

Blooming lilac bushes surrounded the porch with a palpable fragrance. Arwyn sat on the open porch wrapped in blankets, at times receiving teary and whispered condolences, at times sitting in silence. Arrow lay in the simple pine box, covered with lilac flowers and handmade cards placed by friends and loved ones. "Two hours in a funeral home would not have been enough," she declared. Indeed.

After three days those caring for Arrow's body transferred him from the wooden casket to the cardboard coffin. The family then drove him to the crematorium, sent off with love and song by a large group that had spontaneously gathered outside the home that morning. Later in the week a standing-room-only memorial was held in a local church.

Our community had had a real initiation in supporting a family choosing to provide after-death care for their beloved at home. For four years the Threshold Care Circle had quietly and steadily held this possibility as an option, and now there were enough people who knew what to do that a whole network sprang into being in a few hours. I knew I could share Arrow's story with the coroners as an amazing example of what is possible when a family chooses a home funeral.

My comfortable room at the Chula Vista was on the sixth floor with a balcony looking into the treetops and a faint glance of the Wisconsin River through the tall pines. I took a walk around the hotel and conference space, locating where everything was so I could get over my initial confusion before the big day. I stayed up, rearranging my slides one last time. While my presentation wasn't until 3 p.m., I planned to attend the entire conference, which started at 8 a.m. Finally at midnight, I set my alarm for 6:30 a.m. and went to bed.

When the phone rang, I was confused, thinking it was my wake-up call. But when I picked up the phone and heard Susan's voice, immediately apologizing for waking me before my presentation, I knew there had been another death. No one calls with good news at 3 a.m.

It was a newborn. The infant boy, Trillium, was perfect at his 5 p.m. birth, but in the early hours of the morning he began to fade, and his parents rushed him to the hospital where he was pronounced dead. Now the coroner was ordering an autopsy, and the distraught parents were hoping someone could tell them how to refuse this procedure.

"That's the coroner's call," I told Susan. She knew this, but needed me to affirm it before she responded. "Find out where the autopsy will be, what the condition of the body will be, when they can pick him up. These are the questions to focus on now."

After I hung up, I wondered how Susan had found me. I hadn't told anyone the name of the hotel I was staying at, not even my husband. I'd chatted with him online to let him know I'd arrived safely, but all he knew was that I was in Wisconsin Dells and on the sixth floor. He got the 3 a.m. call, too, when they were trying to locate me. He hung up the phone in great relief that *his* family was OK.

I tried unsuccessfully to go back to sleep.

Charlene Elderkin is a hospice volunteer, a home funeral educator, and a member of the National Home Funeral Alliance. She is currently a student of the Chalice of Repose Project in the Contemplative Musicianship Program. Her writing has appeared in *Lilipoh*, *The Correspondence*, *Pea Soup* and *Essential Inklings*.

Photo by Pamela Hale

Ancient ruins in Sacred Valley, Peru.

"In the wake of their deaths, I do not feel absence—but a deep and wide presence.
The gifts from the portal keep coming."

GIFTS FROM THE PORTAL

LAURA WEAVER

Death and life are companions—tango partners strutting across the dance floor of existence. And yet so often in Western culture, death is banished to the shadows, hidden behind closed doors, talked about in hushed voices—as if death were a terrible secret, as if death were something we could hide from if only we knew where to hide. Over a two-year period, I had the heart-wrenching, earth-shattering, and soul-cracking experience of walking with three dear women friends through their deaths from cancer. Each woman danced her own tango with death with tremendous beauty, honesty, and courage. And each woman allowed for the wholeness of her own experience to be witnessed—the terror and peace, the hope and despair, the dismantling of her body, and the luminosity of her spirit.

During those two years, I became well acquainted with blood transfusions and morphine drips; oxygen machines and medical marijuana; the wisdom of hospice nurses and the tender complexity of grief. Death pulled me so close to that portal between here and there that I could hear strange and beautiful music filtering through and smell the scent of the other side on my own skin. Death pulled me so close that I began to see that my avoidance of it had cut me off from some of the juicy bounty of life.

I began to wonder what would happen to us as individuals and a people if we met our lives with a full understanding of how integral dying is to life. How would our world change if we were not constantly running from death's presence? What if we stopped characterizing dying from an illness as a battle lost? What if we allowed ourselves to see beyond the surreal and desensitizing media images of death into the intimate realities of dying? What if we experienced death as a compassionate presence that is with us in every moment—in our own cells and souls, in each other, in our world? What if the angel of death was our guide and mentor instead of our nemesis? It is in the spirit of sharing our truths about death, of opening the door to this forbidden room, that I offer these stories of three women whose lives and deaths transformed my own experience of living.

Sonia

It is late summer, and the foothills are filled with waving grasses gone to seed, the landscape tawny and honeyed. We sit in Sonia's living room, the afternoon sun lighting up her face and the scar on the back of her head.

"It's a snake," I say, startled by the raw beauty of the sinuous jeweled track stitched into her skull.

She laughs, then asks, "What do you think that means?"

"I don't know," I say, shrugging. "Transformation? Shedding your skin?"

She laughs heartily. "Well, I'm certainly doing that."

Sonia is two weeks out from a brain surgery to remove a cancerous tumor. A month ago she had a radical mastectomy to remove her left breast and multiple lymph nodes—the surgery has left her with constant edema and limited range of motion. Her recovery is going smoothly, and yet she knows a long road stretches ahead—chemotherapy, horrendous odds, the unknown—again and again, the unknown. She is a single mother of four children. I watch her two daughters and two sons move through the rooms, a certain look in each of their eyes. They shudder each time the oxygen tank kicks on again.

After they are gone she takes me by the shoulders and asks me, "What if I'm dying? What if I don't make it?" A long pause stretches between us. There is nothing I can say to fill the void of the unknown. She continues. "I just have to take the next step and then the next one. I have no other choice." I take her hand and kiss her fingers, and we sit quietly watching the sun trace squares of light across the walls.

Months pass. Winter comes. Sonia is sitting on her bed, tears streaming down her face.

"I've gotten behind on my surrendering," she says. In the last weeks, her lung has collapsed again and again. The sound of the oxygen tank in her home has become ubiquitous. Chemotherapy has thinned her hair, changed her complexion, stolen her appetite. Some days it is only a bowl of Lucky Charms that she can get down. Over the last few days, a milkshake here and there, a bowl of cereal, a few peanut M&Ms.

I look for authentic words. "Illness brings so much chaos," I say. "You wouldn't be human if you didn't resist, if you weren't afraid. Who is asking you to hold this perfectly? What is perfectly? You read these damn cancer books and they tell you on the one hand not to repress your emotions, especially anger and sadness, but on the other hand maintain a good attitude and positive outlook. What's a woman to do?"

She shrugs and we laugh at the impossibility of it all, the cosmic joke of the whole situation. Laughter is medicine and comes as frequently as the tears these days. Looking into her eyes, I feel the impossible paradoxes death brings. Our organism is programmed to survive—it is the most primary impulse in the body. Its instinct is to hold on. I think of birth—and how contraction and expansion are both essential aspects of labor. What if our resistance is just part of the natural way we move through transitions? What if the resistance is just as essential as our surrender?

It is spring time. Sonia's last. Forsythia. Apple blossoms. Lilacs. Iris. In the last weeks, something has shifted. Knowing she is dying, Sonia is having intimate conversations with each of her children and loved ones to say goodbye.

One day she says to me, "You know, I'm sorry about what happened between us." A year before, we had gone through a period of distance in our friendship. "I don't want to revisit it—because it doesn't matter now, but I just want to acknowledge it. You're here now. I'm here now. That's what matters." I squeeze her hand and thank her, moved by her courage to say the unsayable—to forgive, to seek forgiveness, to reach beyond the boundaries the ego so often imposes in our everyday lives. There are no more old resentments, nothing to hold back.

More and more she is in between. Morphine. Medical marijuana. The pull of that other world. Sitting with her, we swing from deep grief and despair to hysterical laughter and giddiness. The combination of the drugs and the dying process make for wild conversations. She tells me what she sees. In the last weeks, spirits of the dead have begun to visit her. I watch her sense a presence, react to things I cannot see. At one point, she speaks of the healing she is doing for her lineage. It's as if she can feel the bigger web she is part of, the arc of a vast story.

More and more, the rational world crumbles and linear forms of communication fail. Silence, breath, and touch become our potent territory of communion. One morning as I am sitting with her, she grabs my hand hard and whispers urgently to me.

"Where am I going? Who will I become?"

I don't know what to say. How do I answer this with any certainty? "What are you afraid of?" I ask her.

"Annihilation. Total annihilation." I watch her free fall. I watch her sense of self unravel. I can't pull her back from the lip of that precipice. Then her face shifts, and she smiles.

"But it's all love, isn't it? It's all love."

I nod. "Yes," I say. "Yes, it is."

It is the last day of school. Sonia is a schoolteacher, and she earlier told a friend that she would wait to die until school was over so as not to disrupt her children's lives. This was just like her to think of others in this way, even into her death. Through the sheer force of her indomitable will, she would find a way to hold out.

For days now, we have felt Sonia slipping into the other world. Tonight she is breathing heavily, mechanically. Something has happened in the last 24 hours, and her body seems almost vacant. Her sister suspects she has had a stroke. Reluctantly I prepare to go, kissing her on the forehead, feeling this might be the last time.

At seven the next morning, Sonia's sister-in-law comes knocking on my door. "Sonia just passed—please come over and help us." I get up immediately and go to her house—the eastern light flooding her bedroom. There is Sonia— still, no breath, her skin tone and color changing already, her spirit no longer occupying her body. The family is planning a three-day, in-house vigil. They do not want to use a funeral home. Beautifully and tenderly, a small group of women lay Sonia out on a blanket. Then each woman in the circle speaks a line of a poem, dips her cloth in the bowl of water, and bathes this precious body. "I bless this hair that the wind has played with," one woman says, then passes the bowl. "I bless your eyes that have looked on us with love." We pass the washcloth, stroke her hair and face, weep. "I bless these hands that have shaped wonders." When we are complete, we wrap her body in a sheet and lay her in a cardboard coffin with flowers. She will remain here for three days, her body preserved with dry ice. In this particular death rite, it is believed that the body and spirit need three days to fully part ways before the spirit can move freely on the otherworld—unencumbered, complete.

We feel Sonia's spirit hovering nearby as people came to say their good-byes. Throughout the vigil, people move in and out of Sonia's room with songs, praySers, readings, photographs. Children run in and out laughing and playing. Many meet death for the first time here in this room. On the third day, a small group of us gather, cry, celebrate, sing, and send her off with a friend who takes her to the crematorium in a cardboard coffin adorned with flowers and offerings in the back of his Subaru. Later, her ashes will be spread in the nearby mountains. Her memorial will be full of sunflowers, children, and a wild chorus of Abba's "Dancing Queen."

Sarah

Sarah knew she was dying. Somewhere deep inside her she knew. She would look at us in those last months, her gaze drawn from some other place, as if she already held the vast cosmos within her. Through her eyes beamed a sense of galactic time—nebulae, blackholes, just-birthing stars.

When Sarah was first diagnosed with Stage 4 colon cancer in July, she immediately started chemotherapy. At first the chemo worked splendidly—she had a 50 percent reduction in her tumors in two months. But soon after that, something shifted. Perhaps the onslaught of chemotherapy became too much for her immune system or perhaps her body knew it was simply her time to die. The cancer load began to gain momentum and, instead of disappearing, the lesions on her liver multiplied at breakneck speed. She continued to try new treatments, and each week she would simply work to gather enough strength and resilience in her system to go back for the next round.

Today I visit Sarah in the hospital—she has checked herself in for a second time this month for fluids and rehydration. "I need rest," she tells me, her voice hoarse and distant. We eat our soup together, the winter light filtering through the curtains. "It's quiet here," she says, "and nobody is begging me to live, nobody is telling me about the next chemotherapy plan." An hour later a hospice doctor visits us. Kind and tender, she sits with Sarah and tells her what she sees. The treatments aren't working. Perhaps it's time to consider going off the chemotherapy, to focus on your quality of life. My heart is breaking listening to this. No one has been this straight with her. And though we wish it wasn't so, someone is naming what is true, and that is a relief. There is no going back. There is no return. Sarah weeps with terror and relief—no more chemo.

But a day later, she changes her mind. There have been many other conversations. Think about your kids. You have to fight. There's always the hope, the chance—this next treatment. And the next. You can't just give up. And so she starts up again. More chemo. A last try. Maybe, just maybe, it will work.

There is a dark lie in our medical paradigm—a message that if we decide to stop treatment, we are giving up. It is a complex paradox to both hold out for possibilities and miracles without conspiring with the denial of the dying process so that our end-of-life experience becomes a jungle of crises, emergency treatments, tubes and treatments. And yet, watching Sarah, I am struck again and again with a sense of deep humility—how can I know, how can any of us know, what we would choose in those moments? There is no "right" path here. And perhaps the chemo will make a difference. We are in the realm of the unknown. I bow to this. And though my heart aches, I understand that she has to give this one more shot.

A few weeks before Sarah's death, I ask her what she wants of life. She writes back: "I want nothing more than to know that I am one of God's brilliant ideas and that there is nothing I have to do to earn my keep." She is filled with these luminous moments. She is a woman stripped away of all of her outer layers, so that her inner bark shines. And from this place, she can access naked wisdom from some newly accessible reservoir of her soul.

The last round of chemotherapy is overwhelming. Nasty white blisters appear across her face. Her body struggles under the toxic load. Three days before Sarah dies, I go to her house to check in on her before leaving for work. I find her half in, half out of her body with the drugs and disease. She cannot function, and I do my best to help her get to the bathroom, bathe her, brush her hair, dress her, and settle her onto the couch. Then I phone the hospice nurse and describe what is happening. She calls an impromptu home visit meeting with the hospice doctor and social worker. They arrive at the same time as two other friends, and we all sit around Sarah in a circle in her living room trying to take in the reality of what the doctor is saying—she is dying. She has to choose: chemo or hospice. She cannot have hospice care while she is under treatment. "No chemo," Sarah says vehemently, exhausted. "No more chemo." Tears are streaming down all of our faces. No more tubes and procedures and treatments and interventions and tests.

The next day Sarah moves to a hospice center. Here she can get rest and the round-the-clock care she needs. When she arrives at the center, she tells the doctor, "I still want to come home." She is grieving her sons—eight and twelve. "I can't leave my babies."

The next morning, I come to sit with her and immediately feel that something has shifted. Overnight an angel must have visited, for some alchemical grace has transformed her fear. Her face is peaceful, her eyes distant.

"I can't tough it out anymore," she says plainly, clearly.

"I know you can't, honey. You don't have to fight anymore. You can let go. It's okay to let go." Holding her hand, I wash her hot face with a cool cloth and sing to her. Two friends arrive, and we join together and sing wordless melodies. She is no longer eating or drinking. She is being drawn by the pull of the tides of that other world.

Over the next hours, friends and family come and go. The night wears on. A friend and I decide to stay through the night, as we sense that Sarah will pass in the next few hours. About 10:00 p.m., we approach a hospice nurse to ask her what her assessment is of Sarah's condition.

"A few hours at most," she says. "But you never know—sometimes there are surprises. I've seen patients hold on for days if they are waiting to see someone. Don't be fooled. She isn't simply asleep. She is doing very important work now," she says, explaining that many people experience a kind of life review at this stage in their dying.

And then she tells us, "There's another man on the floor who is very close to death. It sounds strange, but we've seen it time and time again—people die in waves. It's as if one person opens the door and a number of souls go through together. My bet is that's what will happen." How beautiful to think that in our dying we shepherd each other across some threshold, that even in this passage we are not alone.

By midnight, my friend and I are exhausted and curl up on the couch in the waiting room to get some rest. At 1:30 a.m. we hear the rush of nurses in the hallway, the announcement that the man down the hall has passed on. We sit up, wide-eyed and awake. We know this man has opened the portal wide, and we wonder if he is waiting for Sarah to join him.

Twenty minutes later, Sarah's sister calls us in to the room. Sarah is in the last stages of her dying—her breathing has changed again and now it comes quickly, erratically. Then again, she shifts, her face softens. She opens her eyes and looks at us, through us, up and to the left, off to some place we cannot follow. Her wide-eyed gaze is penetrating and fierce and full of grace—of this view that is only hers to see. And then minutes later, her breath comes in gasps. We tell her we love her; that it is okay for her to go. And then she simply stops breathing.

Within minutes, we can see that Sarah is no longer present in her body. Her body is like a vacant house with all of its original form but no occupant. And yet watching her, we can also feel that her body is continuing to undergo a process of its own—something is releasing and unwinding. Sarah is here and not here.

As we sit with her body, we feel that door to that other world closing. People come and go and say goodbye. Finally it is just one other friend and I with Sarah. It is strange to be with her like this. Alone. Silent. We keep expecting her to start breathing again. We stay with her over an hour—talk to her and tell her jokes. We feel her presence so strongly it makes the hair on the back of our necks stand on end. And then we sense that it is time for us to go. It is time for *us* to let her go.

Michelle

She wears a short, blonde wig as she greets me on her front porch— her smile as wide and full of light as ever. Her hair is almost gone from the series of chemotherapy treatments she is undergoing. We take a walk along her country road, past the cottonwood trees turning autumn gold, the brook gurgling with just spilled rain, the horses switching their tails in the afternoon light. She shares the news—the doctors have told her that this last round of chemotherapy is no longer working—the cancer has mutated and the old approach is no longer effective—they want to try another concoction. She tells me how in the appointment her husband had pushed back—what if this next treatment doesn't work? Then we'd try another, says the doctor. And after that, if that doesn't work? The doctor pauses and sighs—then it's palliative and hospice care.

Despite the months of chemotherapy she has undergone, Michelle doesn't look or feel sick. Somehow she has retained a vibrancy, a brilliance from the inside out. She does not have the tell-tale ashy gray skin tone that indicates the presence of chemo in the system. As I walk with her, I think—if she is dying, then she's doing it New Orleans style—with pizzazz and vigor, horns blasting and flags flying. If she is getting ready for this next phase of transformation, then she is a caterpillar preparing to build its own jade chrysalis threaded through with this gold that is her soul.

She tells me she cannot even let this latest news into her system—she just can't let it in. She's not sure what she'll do—another round of a different chemo, or take a two month break, see what the tumors do and then make a decision. She is not sure how to make these decisions and yet, somehow, she is walking with such lightness, somehow her smile is absolutely radiant. Perhaps she knows somewhere that illness and dying is not a tragedy—but a part of our agreement with life. Perhaps she has a sense of the bigger story that this cancer journey is part of.

Two weeks ago, she said to me, "Perhaps I am being called to help from the other side—to assist with this rite of passage the planet is in the midst of." Her words struck home. They felt true. Just as we are called to unknown places in life, perhaps we are called for a particular reasons to the other side. But what is the other side? How strange that we can sense this place or state where we arrive from and return to but have so little understanding of it. Walking with Michelle along the road, listening to her news, the words of the hospice nurses echo in my mind: "We couldn't do this job if we didn't know with every fiber of our being that death is not the end."

It is Thanksgiving and Michelle is in constant, chronic hip pain. The pain has etched something different in her face and body—something more uncertain. She wonders if she will ever be the same after this, if her spirits will be restored, or whether her condition will continue to degenerate. First there's the pain, then the pain drugs to manage the pain, then the nausea from the pain drugs, then the anti-nausea medicine that simply knocks her out for hours at a time. She says, within the cauldron of this pain, she is only able to survive moment to moment to moment. Breath to breath. The pain is everything, her world shrinking around it. "When I feel like this, all I want to do is be held," she says, tears welling up in her eyes. She says she can no longer trust her own intuition because there is so much fear. She doesn't know what to do. Doesn't know what's happening. We talk about the force of disintegration—the blasting, overwhelming, undeniable force of disintegration.

A few weeks later, I sit on the edge of Michelle's hospital bed as she receives the second blood transfusion in two weeks. Her eyes are closed and she is so deeply peaceful—the sensory world is becoming too much now. She is listening and speaking from a deep well within. She says the hospice doctor told her she was dying—that she only has a month or two left. She says she doesn't feel like she is dying. If only she can get on top of this pain, things could turn around. She's angry with him, this doctor—she feels he's given her a death sentence. How is she supposed to maintain hope in the face of that prognosis? This is the tension between the possibility of a turnaround and the acceptance of the dying process. How to hold both sides?

Michelle tells me that even though she's angry with this hospice doctor, he has her thinking about closure. She's asks me, "What does closure mean? How do I do it well? Do I need to tell people everything I've ever thought about them? Do I need to share my untold secrets?" As she talks about one friend who she recently had conflict with, she says, "It's funny—I have nothing left to process with him, because now all that is left is love. All the rest has fallen away." The stories that have bound her to this world begin to unravel, to release their hold. I watch her unhook. It is like a sailcloth tearing free.

Michelle knows I have walked with two other friends through death. At one point, she says to me, "I'd like to know what you have learned about death from watching your friends die." I have no idea what I can say about these mysteries. I can only share what I have felt, sensed. How, when the door between worlds swings wide in birth or death, the pulsing, awake, essence-of-being pours through. How, when this portal is open, there is simply this undeniable presence. This knowing is always available to us, and yet, in the threshold moments, it becomes ever more palpable. Finally I speak, try to say something true. "We are held," I finally say. "No matter what, we are always held." But the words feel too small for their meaning. They are mere shadows, pointers.

I wake up knowing this is her day—I simply feel it in my bones. A few hours later I get a call asking me to join another woman at the hospice center to sit vigil. I arrive and immediately see what is happening—Michelle has entered an active dying stage—her breath labored and rattling. My friend and I have to move against our own impulses to keep her alive. Every time her breath becomes ragged, we want to run to the hospice nurse and say, "Fix this, stop the rattling, this isn't right." But this is what death is, this is how it happens—her organs must shut down, and she must stop breathing—this is the way through the portal.

Michelle's eyes are closed and she is deeply inside herself. For days I have felt her engaging in this process of internal alchemy, in which all of her energies are drawn inward to stoke the inner fires. She is transmuting her pain and suffering, she is letting go of this life, this version of herself. She is preparing herself to cross this great threshold. I know she hears and feels us as we sit and stroke her feverish brow, sing to her, whisper to it—it's okay, this is normal, this is just the body letting go.

A friend has called a prayer vigil for 2:00 that afternoon, feeling that Michelle might need the support of a circle of loved ones to help her make this final passage. We will gather in the meeting room down the hall from Michelle's room. In the meantime, we simply witness and support her process—it is like labor and we her doulas. She is moving closer and closer to transition, to the point when the contractions come one on top of the other without any pause between. Sometime in the early afternoon something shifts in her, and we both feel a tidal wave of heat and electricity coming off of her body. It nearly bowls us over. It is the fierce light of fission as body and soul separate. Tremendous waves of energy release, pouring over us in a waterfall of invisible light.

Thirty of us gather in a circle. We start off with prayers—then move to singing. A young woman leads us in a simple rendition of a hallelujah song—just a few chords. We begin gently, slowly. Then the song gains strength and speed and volume. It builds and harmonies interweave, the chorus swelling to a pitch. We can all feel it coming, this crescendo. Michelle's crowning is close. Standing in that circle, I do not even know where my hand ends and another's begins. I am shaking and singing from somewhere I have never sung before. The portal is opening. We are opening it for Michelle and she for us. The view is vast and breathtaking—and what flows through is ecstatic, pure presence. I feel like we all might drop to the floor and begin speaking in tongues. A most primal language is here in the room, and we are all part of its utterance.

Just as the hallelujah song reaches its peak, the hospice nurse comes in, announcing that Michelle has passed, confirming what we have felt. We are all weeping and sweating and trembling—full of this bliss and grief, overwhelmed and bewildered by the blast from the portal that has been thrown open before us. I find myself carried down the hall by some force I do not understand. I find myself in the hospital room where Michelle lays in her bed, her sons beside her. I put my hands on her body and again feel the waves of electricity pouring off her, that sense of fission, of splitting apart, of separation. Her spirit is gone, and yet something is here—all of her memories, all this intelligence that lives in the cells, this deep imprint of consciousness that is embedded in this form. We sit in silence with her. Now she is everywhere, and every corner of the cosmos is singing her name.

I recently heard a story of a woman in a hospice center. She met her dying with full awareness and consciousness of her own dying process—engaging in meditation practice on a daily basis, talking directly about her death with others, and meeting every single day she had left with an open heart. She knew she only had a few months left of life. And yet when she finally entered the hospice center in the heat of summer, she brought a winter coat with her, *just*

in case. Just in case. In the late fall before my friend Sarah died, she bought a bright pair of spring sandals—*just in case.* Perhaps, just perhaps, she would have the chance to walk through her flower garden one last time, to see the poppies bursting open.

I miss the in-the-flesh presence of these women every day and feel their essence informing my life like radiant strands of thread in a tapestry. And though I cannot pick up the phone to call them, they are each available in some very different way. In the wake of their deaths, I do not feel absence—but a deep and wide presence.

The gifts from the portal keep coming. Sometimes it is a flash of a smile, and I think—ah, yes, that's Michelle—and she is encouraging me to leap where I am most afraid. Or I hear a guttural, wild laugh in a crowded room, and I think, oh, yes, thank you Sonia—it is good to laugh—life can be way too serious. Or I am walking along a trail and feel Sarah's presence and think—oh, to be one of God's brilliant ideas for a time on this earth. To know I do not have to earn my keep. To be this, here, now. Let me always remember. Let me never forget.

Laura Weaver, MA is a poet, writer, educator, rites of passage guide, mother, and lover of the wilds. In a very short period of time, her own journey through illness and the experience of walking with three close friends through death brought her into close contact with the mysteries of living and dying. Through that journey, she began to deeply explore the ways threshold experiences of all kinds initiate individual and collective transformation. She received her master's degree in English from the University of Colorado at Boulder and taught English and creative writing for many years before moving into the nonprofit world. Her published poetry and writing can be found in many journals and collections and on her blog www.soulpassages.wordpress.com.

ABOUT THE AUTHOR

Charlene Elderkin volunteers for the Bland Bekkedal Center for Hospice Care in Viroqua, Wisconsin and is a Home Funeral Educator. She cofounded the Threshold Care Circle (2006), one of the first home funeral educational organizations in the Midwest, and is a member of the National Home Funeral Alliance. She is currently a student of the Chalice of Repose Project in the Contemplative Musicianship Program.

Her works on death related topics have been published in *Essential Inklings*, *The Correspondence*, *Lilipoh*, and an advance-planning book co-written with Kathy Neidert, *My Final Wishes*, is available at www.thresholdcarecircle.org. Charlene is an experienced public speaker with audiences ranging from a handful to hundreds. She has written numerous articles and given public presentations on local food and cooperative history while working as marketing manager at the Viroqua Food Cooperative.

In her off-duty life she sings with the RidgeTones, tries not to work too hard in her overly large garden, takes long walks with her husband Nathan, and spends time with her six adult children and three grandchildren.

26192600R00125

Made in the USA
Charleston, SC
27 January 2014